Books by Joan Elma Rahn

SEEING WHAT PLANTS DO
HOW PLANTS TRAVEL
GROCERY STORE BOTANY
MORE ABOUT WHAT PLANTS DO
HOW PLANTS ARE POLLINATED
THE METRIC SYSTEM
ALFALFA, BEANS & CLOVER
GROCERY STORE ZOOLOGY
SEVEN WAYS TO COLLECT PLANTS
WATCH IT GROW, WATCH IT CHANGE
TRAPS AND LURES IN THE LIVING WORLD
EYES AND SEEING
PLANTS THAT CHANGED HISTORY
KEEPING WARM, KEEPING COOL
EARS, HEARING, & BALANCE
MORE PLANTS THAT CHANGED HISTORY
ANIMALS THAT CHANGED HISTORY

A·N·I·M·A·L·S
That Changed History

Joan Elma Rahn

A · N · I · M · A · L · S

That Changed History

ILLUSTRATED BY THE AUTHOR

Atheneum   1986   New York

Copyright © 1986 by Joan Elma Rahn

All rights reserved. No part of this book may be reproduced or transmitted in any form or by any means, electronic or mechanical, including photocopying, recording, or by any information storage and retrieval system, without permission in writing from the publisher.

Atheneum Books for Children
Macmillan Publishing Company
866 Third Avenue, New York, NY 10022

Composition by Heritage Printers, Charlotte, North Carolina
Printed and bound by Fairfield Graphics, Fairfield, Pennsylvania
Designed by Mary Ahern
First Edition

10 9 8 7 6 5 4 3 2 1

Library of Congress Cataloging in Publication Data

Rahn, Joan Elma.
Animals that changed history.

Bibliography: p. 108.
Includes index.
SUMMARY: Discusses the effects on history—for better or worse—made by the horse, rat, and beaver.
1. Animals and civilization—Juvenile literature.
2. Horses—Juvenile literature. 3. Rats as carriers of disease—Juvenile literature. 4. Beavers—Juvenile literature. [1. Animals and civilization. 2. Horses. 3. Rats as carriers of disease. 4. Beavers] I. Title.
QL85.R34   1986   909   86-3635
ISBN 0-689-31137-0

CONTENTS

A·N·I·M·A·L·S
That Changed History

INTRODUCTION

TODAY IS what it is because of the past. What happened in the past has had some influence, big or small, on today's world.

This book tells of several animals that played important roles in history: horses, whose muscular power performed much of the hard work of peace and war throughout nearly all but the most recent history; black rats and fleas, the carriers of the dreaded disease plague, the ravaging illness which, in just a few years, completely changed European society in the mid-1300s; and the American beaver, the greed for whose fur led European traders to explore virtually the whole of Canada.

CHAPTER 1

Horses in History

WILD HORSES ran free ten thousand years ago on the *steppes*—grasslands that extend across much of Asia and into eastern Europe. These horses were relatively short and stocky—something like ponies. They stood only about 13 hands—52 inches (a hand equals 4 inches.)—high at

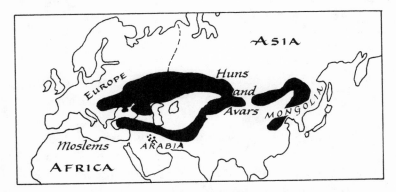

The steppes, or grasslands of central Asia and eastern Europe, are shown in black. Ancient Sumer is indicated by stippling. The dotted line represents the Ural Mountains, which separate Europe and Asia.

*From the medium-sized Mongolian wild horse have
descended all breeds of horses that exist today including
Clydesdales, one of the largest recognized breeds, and
miniature horses raised as pets.*

the withers, which is what the ridge between the shoulder
bones is called. The hairs of their short manes stood up-
right, and they had no forelocks. Their overall color was
yellow dun, but they had a dark mane, its color continuing as a dark stripe along the back to the tail. Tough and
wiry, the horses endured the harsh climate of the steppes
with their hot summers and cold winters.

As these wild horses spread over wide expanses of
Asia and Europe, succeeding generations in different
areas developed characteristics adapted to the conditions

there—the climate, the physical terrain, and the vegetation. Some, for instance, became larger, some slimmer. Their colors, the thickness of their coats, and even the lengths of their manes varied. From these varieties of wild horses, people, years later, were able to develop the many breeds that exist today, which all belong to the same species (*Equus caballus*).

The original type of wild horse in Asia is known today as the Mongolian wild horse; it is also called Przewalski's horse because in 1879, when it had been thought to have become extinct, the Russian explorer Nikolai Przewalski discovered a few small herds of these horses still running wild in Mongolia.

The Mongolian wild horse was never tamed. Those in zoos today refuse to be ridden or trained to harness. The horse that *was* tamed was the *tarpan*, a horse that descended from the Mongolian wild horse and that resembled it very much in size, appearance, and sturdiness, but not in stubbornness.

Early Horsemen

BEFORE RECORDED HISTORY, the people in central Asia had developed an interest in horses—hunting them for food. Horsemeat is nutritious and tastes something like beef. If they could control some mares with young foals, they could also have a valuable addition to their diet—mare's milk. Probably from some half-tamed horses kept for food descended the first horses trained to work for human beings.

No one knows whether people used horses first for riding or for draft purposes (pulling carts and wagons). Both events occurred too far back in time to have been recorded in written history, possibly about 4000 B.C. or a little later. It was not much later than that, that the world's first expert riders and the earliest breeders appeared on the steppes of central Asia. In what today is southern Russia lived the world's first professional horsemen.

They became adept riders and herders. They hunted on horseback. When they planned to be gone all day they usually rode mares, then drank mare's milk or *koumiss* (fermented mare's milk, something like yogurt). These horse-herding people bred their horses for increased size, strength, swiftness, and stamina. As their herds multiplied they came to have ten, perhaps even twenty, horses apiece. At those times when hunting of other animals was poor, the people would bleed a horse—not enough to harm it—and either drink the blood or turn it into a pudding-like food. While the wound was healing, other horses would be bled in turn. In times of great want, a horse might be killed and eaten. The hides of dead horses were used to make clothing and tents.

Knowing the value of their tough, wiry horses, these people became nomads, driving the animals to the best pastures. As one pastureland became overgrazed, they moved on to another, taking their homes and possessions with them. The horses carried these burdens on their backs or pulled them in carts.

The nomads and their herds frequently prospered,

but sometimes an overpopulation problem among both people and horses occurred. Then the nomadic tribes, swifter and stronger than the agricultural peoples who led a sedentary life and had little use for horses yet, would descend on farming villages and kill most of the inhabitants and either destroy or take for their own any of the farmers' possessions they wanted—including the land. This sort of thing was to recur many times in history, and the fighting nomadic horsemen of Asia came to strike fear into the hearts of not only their fellow Asians, but later of Europeans as well. The horse had become a companion of human beings in war as well as in peace.

War Chariots of the Ancient World

THE NATURAL HABITAT of wild horses did not extend to southwestern Asia, which is mostly desert. There they were unknown until the ancient Sumerians (living in what is present-day Iraq) learned of horses from the central Asian tribes about 3500 B.C. The Sumerians had already trained the *onager* (a trainable, but very stubborn near-relative of the horse) to pull war chariots, but they found the horse easier to handle.

The war chariot was a two-wheeled or four-wheeled cart designed to hold one to three men. Either one man served as both driver and swordsman, or the swordsman had a driver and perhaps an additional man to protect him with a shield. Not all the work of war was done by the men, however.

Hitched four abreast to the chariots, the horses must

Ancient civilizations of the Middle East used horses to draw war and hunting chariots. The harness was an inefficient one, for the strap around the horse's neck tended to choke it as it pulled a weight behind it. This was one reason why several horses were used to pull a light chariot.

have been a terrifying sight to any enemy on which they advanced. Their function was to trample as many enemy foot soldiers as possible. The swordsman later cut off the heads of the dead or dying.

The war chariot had one disadvantage. It was useful only in flat country. Chariots were likely to be wrecked on irregular ground and to run over their own horses on a steep descent. On a steep ascent, the primitive harnessing used by ancient peoples was likely to choke the horses. With this is mind, people who expected to be the objects of attacks by chariots built their fortresses on hills—reducing the chariot's effectiveness as a weapon.

In light of all this, it took only one simple invention

to free the war horse of his chariot—and to put the fighting man firmly on his back.

The Stirrup Changes War

IT WAS SUCH a small thing and so simple a thing, probably invented for the comfort and convenience of the rider. It was, however, to change the way people conducted themselves in both war and peace for a couple of thousand years. That invention was the *stirrup*.

The first riders had ridden bareback, their knees holding tightly to the horse's body. Only with a gentle horse proceeding at a slow pace could a rider let his legs relax. Later, riders put a cloth or piece of hide, sometimes padded, on the horse's back. The cloth was held in place by a strap that went around the horse's body. Such a simple saddle may have given a slightly softer ride, but the rider still had to hang on largely by gripping with his knees. This was especially true if the rider's hands were occupied with weapons to be used in hunting or war.

The first stirrups almost certainly were an invention of the horsemen of central Asia—probably no later than 300 B.C. They gave the rider a more secure seat on his horse. He could rest part of his weight on the stirrups, which could be made to a length suitable for his legs, or, if he wished, the rider could stand in the stirrups. It was this greater security on horseback offered by stirrups that made the mounted warrior a more formidable foe than he had ever been before.

Until stirrups came into use, the function of a horse

ridden into battle was largely to take his rider quickly where he wanted to go to fight and then to get him out of danger. A rider without stirrups could not brandish his weapons any more fiercely than could a soldier on foot. Hanging on by his knees, a warrior did not dare to swing his sword or club with too much vigor for fear that he might upset his balance and fall from his horse. Once dismounted, he had lost his means of swift transportation and was at the mercy of any mounted enemy soldiers.

With the more secure seat that stirrups provided, the rider could apply his weapons with greater force without fear of throwing himself off his own saddle. In addition, with the rider firmly seated, he and the horse in some sense became as one living thing. Not only was the rider's strength applied to a blow toward the enemy, but the combined force of a horse and its rider rushing forward made the blows even more devastating.

If one firmly mounted man could do such damage, an army of such men was a force to be reckoned with. The day of the massed mounted cavalry had come. The Asian horsemen who used stirrups soon became the scourge not only of Asia, but of Europe as well. Several times in the course of history a well-organized army of expert cavalry swept out of the east into Europe. They usually followed the grasslands north of the Caspian Sea and the Black Sea and penetrated to the forests of western Europe. One of these groups, the Huns, were Mongols whose terrifyingly swift raids, beginning about A.D. 370, left such an impression on Europe that their name is still used in a disparaging way to characterize any destructive people.

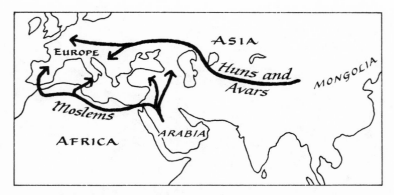

The routes by which several stirrup-using armies invaded Europe.

The Avars, also a Mongolian people, invaded Europe about A.D. 560. A completely different group, Moslems, originally from Arabia, invaded Spain from North Africa in A.D. 711. All three of these peoples were eventually driven out of Europe, but not before they had left a legacy—each had brought its own version of the stirrup. By the mid-700s, at least some horsemen in western Europe were using it.

As the use of the stirrup made weapons more formidable, the need for better protection from them increased. Fighting men, of course, had always sought to protect their bodies from their enemies' blows. Many carried shields of thick leather or of metal. Some wore shirts of thick leather, but these could be stiff and confining. Body armor made of small overlapping pieces of leather or metal in a "fish-scale" arrangement was more flexible, as were later garments made of *chain mail*. Chain mail consisted of metal rings linked together to form a sort of metal "cloth."

With the exception of a small opening for vision, a knight in full armor was completely encased in metal. He often used a lance to attack an enemy, and he carried a shield for additional protection from his opponent's lance.

These forms of armor provided moderately good protection from many blows received from foot soldiers or from stirrupless riders. They could not, however, prevent the entrance of sharply pointed objects presented with great force—as from a rider in stirrups—nor could they prevent internal injuries from a really smashing blow from a club wielded by a rider in stirrups. Knights, the fighting men of Europe in the Middle Ages, began to wear solid armor. In the 1100s and 1200s, small pieces, such as metal caps and breastplates, protected only certain especially vulnerable parts of the body. Later, as metalworkers became more skilled, they encased the knight's body in plates of metal cut and hinged so smoothly as to make strong but flexible suits of armor. By the 1500s knights usually wore full suits of heavy plate armor made to order to suit their personal tastes.

All the protection that full plate armor could afford was needed, for the stirrup had led to the more efficient employment of a simple weapon that had already been in use. Originally the *lance* was only somewhat longer than the sword. Unlike the sword it had no cutting edges but ended in a point. As the lance was first used, a warrior brandished it either overhand or underhand at an enemy in an attempt to run the point into a vulnerable part of his body. It might have been thrown, in which case it had to be retrieved. It was better, though, to come close enough to impale the enemy while still keeping a grasp on the handle; that way the lance could be removed quickly and be available for reuse immediately.

With the coming of the stirrup, the use of the lance changed. The lance became longer, and the knight held it firmly between his upper arm and his body. Some suits of plate armor even had a little projection against which he could brace his lance. Then, as he and his horse charged forward, the rider aimed the tip of the lance at the face or chest of his opponent. With the force of the galloping horse behind it, the well-aimed lance usually went straight through the body of a man wearing only chain mail. The protection of plate armor thus became almost a necessity.

Even with plate armor, the force of a well-aimed lance might topple a knight from the saddle. One solu-

A knight's destrier (a great horse trained for battle) was also protected by armor. Except for the biblike covering of chain mail around his neck, the rest of the horse's armor is metal plate including the jointed plates that allow him to bend his neck. The curves of the armor directed some blows away from the nose and legs.

tion was to shape the body armor so that a blow was likely to glance off it. Another was to build up the front and back of the saddle so that the saddle encased the lower part of the knight's body; there was just room enough for his legs to extend out on either side. With the armored knight firmly held in the saddle and with the saddle firmly fitted on the horse, it was the horse that took much of the brunt of well-placed blows delivered to his rider.

It had long been obvious—probably from the first day that an aggressive rider on horseback had victimized another person—that killing or disabling the horse would greatly reduce the fighting power of the rider. This was especially true when the rider wore a complete suit of plate armor. The dismounted wearer of chain mail could still move about more or less nimbly on his feet and mount another horse. When suits of armor were at their greatest weight, a knight could hardly walk in his suit of armor and could not rise from the ground if he had fallen in a prone position. Neither could he mount a horse unaided. Once dismounted in the midst of battle, he was likely either to be killed or to be taken prisoner and held for ransom.

It was important, therefore, to injure the enemy's horse while protecting one's own. Therefore, horses going into battle often wore armor similar to that of their riders. At first they wore leather, then chain mail, and finally plate armor.

A horse wearing full plate armor and carrying a fully armored knight carried a burden of at least 400 pounds. To bear all this weight, the horse had to be strong and at least moderately large. Although the descendants of the horses originally used by ancient horsemen had been bred to a somewhat larger size than the Mongolian wild horse, the people of northern Europe had had at their disposal a variety of wild horse that was larger than the wild horses of central Asia. By breeding these and in each generation using the largest animals for continued breeding, they were able to develop a large, heavily muscled horse that could carry the weight of a rider and armor. The largest of them were called *great horses.*

The weight of a great horse, his rider, and the two sets of full armor had another important effect—it made the combined horse-rider a formidable weapon. It took some urging to get the heavily burdened horse into action, and the horse was not capable of maintaining a gallop for very long. However, once the animal achieved a full gallop it was impossible for him to stop quickly. Neither could he make sharp turns. The horse-rider combination proceeded forward something like a tank today—it trampled everying in its path and was not highly maneuverable. But the lance, with all that weight behind it proceeding at full gallop, could hit with tremendous force when it found its target. In fact, lances came to be made with crossbars just behind the point so that a lance would not penetrate so deeply into an enemy's body that the knight could not pull it out quickly.

When called upon to protect his homeland or king, a knight did not simply mount his horse, ride to wherever battle was about to occur, and then proceed to fight. Un-

A lance was a devastating weapon when carried by a fully-armored knight on a galloping horse.

less he was a young man just starting his career or a knight somehow down on his luck, he usually traveled with at least three horses of his own and a retinue of several persons that served him and cared for his horses and their own as well.

A knight never traveled on the back of his war horse, a great horse called a *destrier*, and he never traveled in his armor. That would have been much too uncomfortable. He rode instead on a *palfrey*, a horse trained to *pace* or *amble*. Most four-legged animals, including most horses, walk by picking up one leg at a time and alternating individual hindlegs and forelegs, left and right legs thus: left hind, left fore, right hind, right fore. A few four-legged animals move with both left legs at the same time and then both right legs at the same time. This is called pacing at fast speed and ambling at low speed. Palfreys had a natural tendency to do this and so could be easily trained to do it. This made for a much more comfortable ride. The knight rode on his palfrey to within a safe distance of the expected battle, then put on his armor, mounted his destrier, and entered the battle.

The knight needed at least one *sumpter* horse (pack horse) to carry his armor, weapons, and other items, and he needed at least one squire to help him dress and to take care of the horses and equipment. And, of course, the squire needed his own horse on which to ride.

A palfrey paced or ambled with both feet on the same side moving at nearly the same time.

This was about the size of a minimum retinue, but some knights went accompanied by archers and some foot soldiers as well, additional personal servants, and additional personal baggage—all of which required more horses.

All this was very expensive. (Just having a properly trained destrier was beyond the means of most people.) Very few men would go to this expense and risk their lives in battle without expecting something in return. Beginning about the 700s, in western Europe the expected reward usually was knighthood and land. The king would knight the men who had supported him in battle and would grant each one a large tract of land.

For the land to be useful to him, the knight had to grow crops on it. It was, of course, below the dignity of a knight to do this himself, and so he needed many people to perform the hard labor. This led to a system called the *feudal system.*

The Feudal System Rises and Falls

UNDER THE FEUDAL SYSTEM, nearly all of society was divided into three groups: the nobility, which consisted of knights who protected the people and the land from invaders; the peasants, who worked the land owned by the knights and raised crops on it; and the clergy, who saw to the spiritual welfare of all Christians. There were, in addition, some people who did not fit into any of these three classes. These were mostly people who had what we would now call middle-class occupations (lawyers, phy-

sicians, shopkeepers, for example), but these were few
in number.

The vast majority of the people were peasants who
knew little else than farming. Hardly any of them could
read or write. Under the feudal system they had traded
their personal freedom and the personal ownership of
land for the protection afforded them by the knights
whose duty it was to go to war or to right injustices.

The peasants had become *serfs*. Serfs were not slaves,
but neither were they entirely free. They were not owned
by another person as a slave was, but in exchange for the
protection of the knights—who were now their *landlords*,
or simply, *lords*—they were required to work a certain
number of days on their lord's land, or *manor*.

Although the details differed from time to time and
from country to country—and even from one manor to
the next—each manor usually had one section of land (the
lord's domain) on which the lord's crops and animals
were raised, a village in which the serfs lived in small
cottages, fields in which the serfs were assigned plots of
ground on which they might grow their own food, and a
forested area at least some of which was reserved for the
lord's private hunting parties and from some of which
serfs were allowed to gather firewood. In the early days
of feudalism very little money ever exchanged hands.
The lords and the serfs merely provided services for each
other—the serfs did the hard everyday labor, and the lords
risked their lives whenever it became necessary to protect the country.

Although serfs were not owned by their lords, they

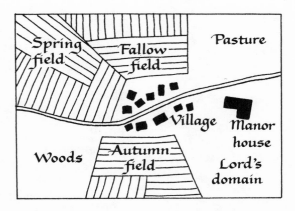

A possible arrangement of land on a feudal manor. Rather than having a single plot of ground, each serf had several strips— not necessarily side by side—in each of the three fields.

had little freedom. Working hours were long and hard. The serfs were usually required to look after their lord's crops before their own. They were often required to obtain their lord's permission before marrying, especially if the marriage were to be with someone from a different manor, for this would mean that one of the lords would lose a serf and the other would gain one plus any children that would come of that marriage. If an independently minded serf did choose to leave his lord's manor, the chances were that he would be forcibly returned. In actual practice, most serfs were bound to the place they were born.

Although life was hard for the peasants living under feudalism, the weather in Europe in early feudal times

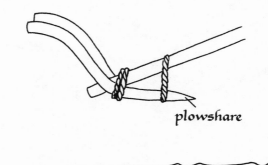

plowshare

The scratch plow was suited to the dry soils of southern Europe. Basically it was nothing but a pointed stick (the point is the plowshare) which was drawn through the soil. Two handles made it easier to control, and it was usually pulled by a pair of oxen.

was generally mild and good for agriculture. The population grew slowly but steadily then, in part because of the favorable weather and in part because of the role that the great horse played in agriculture as well as in war.

Farming in Europe had originated in the south where the weather was drier and the soils were finer than in the north. Such soil was easy to plow with simple *scratch plows* pulled by oxen, rarely horses. The damp, heavy northern soils were more difficult to plow. The *heavy plow*, invented for this type of soil, cut out thick ribbons of soil and turned them over. This required strong animals to pull the plow. The great horses, with their strength and size, originally bred for war, partially solved this problem, but that was not enough.

One reason the horse had not been used for plowing earlier was that efficient harnessing for horses had not been invented. Very early in ancient times people had tried a simple collar around the horse's neck. When the horse pulled against the collar, it squeezed against his windpipe and the major arteries in his neck. With both his wind and his blood supply to the brain partially cut off, the horse could not work efficiently. An early improvement—a harness with a breastband against which the horse pulled—helped, but even the breastband pressed somewhat against the windpipe and arteries. A pair of horses with this type of harness simply could not plow as much land as a pair of oxen pulling against their yoke. Some time well before A.D. 1000 some unknown person invented the *horse collar*. The thick, firm collar rested

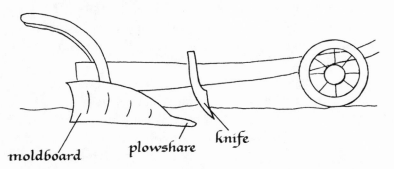

moldboard   plowshare   knife

The heavy plow used in the damp, northern soils had a knife that sliced through the soil just ahead of the plowshare. Attached to the plowshare was a curved moldboard. The combined plowshare-moldboard cut the soil and turned it over. Wheels made the heavy plow easier to handle.

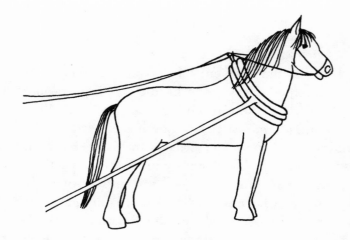

The rigid horse collar rested on the horse's shoulders and allowed him to pull a heavy load without strangling himself. (Compare with the ancient harnessing shown on page 10.)

against the horse's shoulders. The horse could lean against it without cutting off his air and blood supply. This way he could use most of his strength to pull the heavy plow. Even so, several great horses were used to pull one heavy plow.

The heavy, damp soils of northern Europe also caused the rapid softening and wearing down of unprotected horses' hooves. Most horses of southern Europe had not been shod, though the Romans had used leather or metal plates tied, something like sandals, to horses' hooves that were subject to wear on paved roads; these shoes must have worn out quickly. Later, metal shoes were clamped onto horses' hooves. Still later, when someone learned that most of the hoof is made of material not sensitive to pain—like your fingernails—horseshoes were nailed to hooves. Although a *nailed horseshoe* could come off, it was less likely to do so in damp soil than one clamped to the hoof.

In northern Europe, great horses, equipped with horse collars, and nailed horseshoes and pulling the heavy plows, could plow more land in a day than could oxen. This made it possible for the peasants there to shift from the old two-field system of crop rotation to a three-field system, and the three-field system helped to support the great horse.

In the old, two-field system, which had been practiced for many years in southern Europe, the crop land on a manor was divided into two roughly equal fields. Each year a crop was raised in one field and the other was allowed to lie fallow (that is, no crop was raised there). On alternate years a field was used for crops and then left fallow. Fallowing allowed a field to regain some of its fertility. During part of the year, farm animals were allowed to graze on the fallow field, their manure adding fertilizer to the soil.

In the three-field system, the land was divided into three portions. Each year about one third of the land was used to raise a winter crop, one third to raise a summer crop, and one third to lie fallow. The winter crop was a cereal grain—winter wheat or rye—planted in the autumn; it sprouted in the autumn, then the seedlings stopped growing but remained alive over winter and resumed growing early the following spring, and the crop was harvested in spring. The summer crop was either a legume (some kind of bean or pea, which enriched the soil with nitrogen as well as providing food), other vegetables, or oats (one of the best foods for horses). The use of the different fields was rotated over a three-year cycle.

In this system, two thirds of the fields rather than only one half were in production at any one time. The planting and harvesting times of the two different crops were different, and so the people's and the horses' work times were spread more efficiently over the year. In addition, it meant that more land was brought into cultivation. Over the years, more of the forests were cut down and more of the swampy areas were drained for cultivation. Both the human population and the farm-horse population grew, creating both the possibility of and the need for expanding still more of the area of land under cultivation.

For several hundred years the feudal system flourished in Europe, but over a few hundred more years it slowly began to disintegrate. The system probably would have died of its own accord as the difference between the members of the relatively few, very rich ruling class and the many poor, hard-working serfs grew to proportions that the serfs would not have tolerated. Other factors, however, helped to hasten the demise of the feudal system.

One of these was the sudden decline in the population when the Black Death, the worst epidemic ever known to strike Europe, devastated that continent in the mid-1300s. Because the Black Death is described in the next chapter, no more about it will be said here.

Other factors included the invention of new battlefield weapons. The crossbow, which was used in Europe as early as the 900s, could penetrate plate armor and was considered so terrible that, in 1139, the church condemned it as unfit for Christians to use against Christians. The Welsh longbow was even more deadly. The arrows shot from a great distance could kill either knight or horse no matter how heavily armored. These weapons alone probably would have doomed the armored knight, but they too were replaced by a completely different invention—gunpowder.

Gunpowder, which probably had been invented by the Chinese about A.D. 900, was available in Europe by

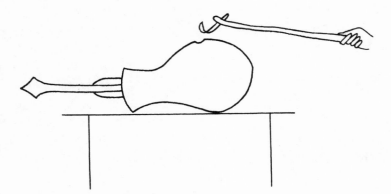

The earliest cannons shot arrows. The cannon contained gunpowder that was lit by a burning fuse placed at a small opening. Such a crude cannon probably did little more damage to the enemy than other weapons of the time, but it was the ancestor of later cannons and handguns, which shot cannonballs or bullets with deadly effect.

the 1200s, but it took a while before it came into general use on the battlefield. People had to learn how to use it safely. The early cannons were small but all too often they exploded and killed the persons firing them rather than the person at which they were aimed. With time, however, they became more reliable. By the 1600s, huge cannons required teams of great horses to pull them to the battlefield, and individual soldiers carried smaller handguns, like muskets and pistols.

Plate armor was no defense against cannonballs, though it might sometimes deflect bullets. It was not advisable to ride straight forward on a big, poorly maneuverable horse toward someone who could kill you from a distance. With the coming of gunpowder to the battlefield, it was much better to have a lighter, more agile horse trained to do some fancy footwork when the occasion demanded.

The armored knight was doomed, and so was the feudal society based on him and his great destrier. The horse, however, was not. Though no longer needed as mounts for knights, the great horses continued to be used for farm work and other draft purposes. Over the years they were bred to even a larger size.

Roads Improve

WELL INTO THE 1500s, people traveling by land either rode on horseback (if they were wealthy enough to afford a horse), or they walked. They rarely rode any long distance in a wagon. This was in part because riding on horseback was associated with knighthood. Any able-bodied person would have been embarrassed to ride in a wagon when he or she was capable of sitting on a horse. Being carried in a vehicle pulled by a horse was considered appropriate only for the sick or injured or for the very young or very old.

Another reason was that most roads were in very poor condition most of the time. In wet weather, a wagon would become bogged down in mud; then passengers had to get out and help push the wagon. When the mud dried, the ruts left there would, at the very least, produce a jarring ride for anyone in a wagon and might cause an axle to break or the loss of a wheel. Horses, of course, pulled wagonloads of equipment or crops on the manors and to nearby towns on market day, but long-distance travel by horse-drawn vehicles was uncomfortable and rare.

Then, in the 1500s, coaches (named for the Hungarian town of Kocs, where they are believed to have originated) began to be used for short distances. These were heavy, rather cumbersome, lumbering vehicles drawn by six to eight great horses. By the 1600s, it was fashionable for wealthy families to ride about in their own coaches. In towns, enterprising people set up their own businesses offering rides to people who did not own their own horses or coaches. Soon, where roads were reasonably good, coaches began to run with some regularity between nearby towns.

About the mid-1600s, a new form of transportation appeared—the stagecoach. A *stage* was a station or stopping place where tired horses were exchanged for fresh

A horse-drawn coach of the 1500s. It had no springs and was open to weather, yet it must have been the best available then. It belonged to Queen Elizabeth I of England.

ones. Hence the name *stagecoach*. Several stations were set up at suitable locations along the road between distant cities. Because fresh horses replaced tired ones at each station, there was no need for long rest periods that would have to be taken if the same horses had pulled a coach the entire length of its journey. Traveling by stagecoach was, for its time, a new form of rapid, long-distance travel, though by our standards it would seem slow as the great horses plodded from station to station.

In the 1700s, roads had improved to the point that lighter coaches drawn by lighter horses could travel faster along the highways. In 1784, the stagecoach carried the mails the 100 miles from London to Bath in only fifteen hours. Coaches now were suspended on springs, which gave passengers a more comfortable ride.

As the 1800s approached, it became fashionable to ride in one's own carriage drawn by sleek, handsome horses. In the early 1800s, coaches pulled by horses ran

A stagecoach of the 1700s offered a somewhat more comfortable ride than Queen Elizabeth's coach.

on rails laid between some cities. These first railroads gave a smoother ride than was available on an ordinary road, and the horses could pull a heavier load.

Soon after this the steam locomotive was invented, and by the mid-1800s it replaced horses on the railroads. This did not lead to a lowered demand for horses, however. As more people traveled by locomotive between cities, there was a rising need for the travelers to be driven between homes and the railway stations. Cities were growing in size, too, and light, horse-drawn cabs carried people within cities.

Horses in America

WHEN CHRISTOPHER COLUMBUS discovered America in 1492, horses were unknown to the inhabitants there. Soon after his first voyage, several Spanish expeditions brought horses to the islands off North America, and on March 12, 1519, sixteen horses reached North America when Hernando Cortes landed in Mexico. (The next day there were seventeen horses; a mare had given birth.)

Cortes and his small army of about 550 men are famous for having conquered the entire Aztec Empire in what is now Mexico. One theory has it that the Aztec Indians, never before having seen horses, thought that a horse and its rider were one strange, two-headed animal, and that the Aztecs' terror at seeing these monsters gave the Spaniards an immediate and lasting advantage over them. This is hardly likely, however. Even though the first sight of a horse and rider must have amazed and startled the Aztecs, they must very soon have seen a Spaniard dismount, and the idea of the monstrous animals would have been proven false.

What defeated the Indians throughout the Americas was almost certainly the diseases that Europeans brought with them and not horses. In fact, Indians saw the value of horses almost right from the start. They acquired horses from Europeans whenever the opportunity presented itself—by buying or stealing them, or by appropriating abandoned animals. In 1542, when the Spaniard Hernando DeSoto was exploring the lower Mississippi River, his expedition had to abandon twenty-two horses. They, and other horses brought later, multiplied on the great grasslands of North America called *prairies*. The prairies stretched all the way up the middle of the United States and into Canada. Here the descendants of these horses became the famous wild mustangs of the American West.

The prairies, or grasslands of North America.

Horses changed the lives of the Plains Indians of North America. In a remarkably short time they, like the ancient peoples of central Asia, became expert horsemen and some of them developed a nomadic existence in which they followed the migrating herds of bison (often erroneously called buffalo). On horseback a man could easily chase down and kill a bison that would provide his family with enough meat for days.

As Europeans occupied more and more of America, horses came with them and provided most of the power needed for the hard work of developing a new country. As in Europe, the horse was early used for riding and as a pack animal. Roads, at first, were nonexistent; then they were often impassable. But as roads improved, horses pulled wagons and coaches between towns. Later, they pulled boats along canals and coaches along early railroads.

Perhaps the most exciting tales of horses in the history of the United States are those told in connection with the tending and driving of great herds of cattle by cowboys and the delivery of mail by the Pony Express. Both of these have been immortalized in Western movies. Although most people are not aware of it, both were short-lived phases of the American past.

The great prairies of the United States were just as suitable for cattle as they were for horses and bison. During the early development of the United States, these grasslands, in the center of the continent, were too far from the great centers of human population on the East and West Coasts. Cattle driven such long distances would have lost weight and would have been too thin for slaughter when they reached the market—if, indeed, they had not died of exhaustion before then. Before the coming of the railroads, there were great herds of cattle on the Texas prairies, but these cattle were raised only for their tallow and their hides, which were tanned into leather. The cowboys ate all the beef they wanted, but the rest of the meat from the slaughtered cattle went to waste.

When, in the 1860s, the first locomotive railroads reached the Mississippi River and began to extend westward, it became feasible to drive fattened cattle from Texas to the railheads at Kansas City, Dodge City, and Abilene. This was the beginning of the great cattle drives for which the American West is famous. It was made possible by the fact that the cowboys rode horses that could outrun and outmaneuver the cattle, which were inclined to stampede when the least thing frightened them.

During a cattle drive each cowboy needed a number of horses, usually about ten. On the open range, the horses ate only what they grazed from the land. Without grain

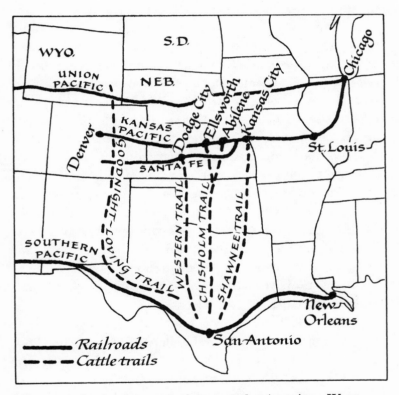

Routes of the famous cattle drives of the American West and the early railroads that crossed the United States.

in their diet, they could work only two or three hours a day and then had to be rested. If they became footsore from too much work on hard or rocky ground, they might require two or three days of rest before working again. For these reasons plenty of spare horses were needed. In addition, some horses were trained for special tasks, such as cutting certain cattle for roping. Some were used only for night work.

Even these cattle drives were long enough to cause cattle to lose enough weight that they lost some of their potential value before they reached the railroads. For this reason, some cattlemen began to drive calves northward from Texas as soon as they were old enough to travel to the grasslands of eastern Wyoming, western Nebraska, or farther north. There the cattle grazed until they reached marketable size and then were driven the short distance to the nearest railroads.

The great cattle drives lasted only about twenty years. By the 1880s, the railroads had become so successful that more lines crossed the country. The Southern Pacific Railroad, which went through the heart of Texas cattle country, was completed in 1883. It was no longer necessary to drive cattle to the railroads; the rails had come to the cattle.

Even shorter-lived was one of the most glamorized bits of American history—the Pony Express. By 1860, there were so many people on the West Coast (drawn mostly by the discovery of gold in California in 1849) that there was a need for rapid communication between the two coasts, but much of the intervening territory was

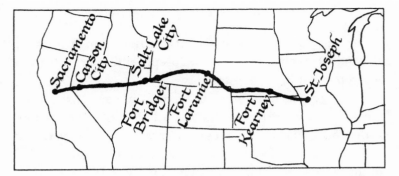

The route of the Pony Express.

either desolate desert or was occupied by Indians, many of whom were understandably hostile to any more intrusion on their lands. It was at this time that a private mail service, the Pony Express, began delivering mail across the nearly two thousand miles between St. Joseph, Missouri, and Sacramento, California. Along the way there were 150 stations roughly ten miles apart. The exact distance depended on the terrain. It was the distance that a good horse could run at high speed before noticeably slowing down.

The company bought over 400 of the best horses it could find for this purpose and distributed them along the stations. Eighty young, short, slim men were hired. Each was to ride about sixty or seventy miles at top speed, stopping every hour or so for only two minutes at a station to sling the mail bags—which were especially fitted for the lightweight saddles the horses wore—onto a fresh horse, perhaps refresh himself with a piece of bread or a cup of coffee, and then he was off. At the end of his run he passed the mail bags on to a waiting rider who carried them for another sixty or seventy miles. In good weather the mail traveled between St. Joseph and Sacramento in the remarkable time of ten days.

There was only one run of mail in each direction a week, so each horse usually got a long rest after its ten-mile dash. The horses received good care and were fed grain, which gave them better endurance than the Indians' horses. This may have saved many a Pony Express-man's life, for his horse usually was able to outrun attacking Indians. Because most horses traveled back and forth on the same route, they usually knew their routes as well as their riders did. On one or two occasions, when its rider had been killed, a horse brought the mail in alone.

The Pony Express began business on April 3, 1860, and it lasted only eighteen months. It was a good service and might have lasted longer, but a new invention, the telegraph, put an end to it. Once telegraph wires were strung across the United States, urgent messages could travel instantly by wire, and less urgent ones could go the slower way by stagecoach or railroad.

It might seem that inventions like locomotives, automobiles, airplanes, telegraph, and telephones would have put horses completely out of work. True, none of us travels by stagecoach or expects the bread to be delivered in a horse-drawn bakery wagon, but today throughout the world there are more than 200 breeds of horses, nearly all of them bred and maintained for a particular purpose.

In the more affluent countries horses are used for pleasure—for riding, racing, or show purposes (including the pulling of brewery wagons by great horses). Some horses earn their living as the mounts of forest rangers or mounted policemen; the horse gives its rider an air of authority that a person on foot does not have. Horses are still used to herd some cattle and other animals raised on the open range.

In a small way, the use of great horses on farms is returning. It began, in part, because of the oil crisis of 1973. Some farmers felt it was more economical to feed horses than to buy fuel for tractors. In addition, horses, in contrast to tractors, have the advantages of providing free manure, being pollution free, and reproducing themselves. It may be that we will see more work horses in the future.

CHAPTER 2

Rats, Fleas, and the Black Death

IT CAME FROM THE EAST. It was invisible, but it cut a path of death and suffering so dreadful that many believed it was the beginning of the end of the world. Some called it the Great Dying, others the Great Pestilence, but later generations gave it a name that reflected the horror and terror of those who had experienced it: the Black Death.

The Black Death was an epidemic of plague that swept across western Europe between 1347 and 1351, a time when medical knowledge was so meager that no one knew about bacteria or about the fact that some bacteria could cause disease. No one knew that both rats and people might be susceptible to some of the same diseases, or that fleas could transmit diseases from rats to human beings. Without such knowledge, there was no intelligent way that people could protect themselves from this epidemic, and the Black Death was the most virulent, most widespread epidemic that Europe had ever experienced.

Plague

PLAGUE IS A DISEASE caused by a *bacillus* (plural, *bacilli*) or rod-shaped bacterium with the scientific name *Yersinia pestis*. (It was formerly called *Pasteurella pestis*, and still earlier *Bacillus pestis*.) Under ordinary conditions—when no epidemic of plague exists among the human population—*Yersinia pestis* is more or less confined to populations of wild rodents that live in large underground colonies in certain areas of the world (the prairie dogs and ground squirrels of the western United States or the marmots of the Asian steppes, for instance). As long as people and their domestic animals stay away from plague-infected colonies of wild rodents, the disease usually remains confined to the wild populations, where it is not so serious a disease as it is in human beings or rats.

If, however, people move among such wild rodent colonies—camping near their burrows or hunting them, for instance—fleas may jump from rodent to human being. If a flea carrying the plague bacilli bites the human being, it may inject some of the bacilli into him. Then it is very likely that the person will become ill with plague. Without proper medical care, his chances of dying are greater than those of surviving.

Unfortunate as this is, such a single event usually does not lead to an epidemic among human beings. Such an epidemic is ordinarily preceded by a plague epidemic among some other species of animal closely associated with human populations, especially the rat, and most especially the black rat (*Rattus rattus*), also called the ship rat and the roof rat.

The black rat.

A long time ago, the black rat, a native of southeastern Asia, adapted to living with human beings—in their houses, barns, and other buildings, and also on board ships. Black rats will eat anything that people or their domestic animals eat; anywhere that people have stored food or deposited their garbage the black rat can find a satisfactory meal. In the Middle Ages, as a matter of course, the common people lived under unsanitary conditions that would shock us today. Farmhouses usually had just one room in which the entire family slept, along with any farm animals that needed shelter. Garbage, as well as both human and animal waste, was not far away. In cities, people merely threw such wastes out the window with or without a warning to passersby below. In addition, most people roofed their houses with thatch (straw); this made cosy nesting material for black rats, which are excellent climbers and had no trouble reaching the roof. The average home of the Middle Ages must have been a paradise for black rats. By then the black rat had ceased being a truly wild animal and occupied human habitations much as dandelions live in lawns today—not really wanted but hard to get rid of and therefore often tolerated.

Although the black rat originated in southeastern Asia, it did not remain there. It is true that black rats do not migrate—they rarely walk more than 200 yards away from their homes—but they will enter containers of food or climb up the ropes securing docked ships and so be transported by human beings for many miles. Consequently, from Southeast Asia they went wherever people went. They especially followed the trade routes, either the caravan routes across Asia or the shipping routes in the Indian Ocean. Some of that trade was in grain or other foods. A rat that got into a sack of grain was carried wherever the grain went. With free food and free transportation, it might travel, plump and well fed, dozens or hundreds of miles in a few days. In this way, black rats eventually spread to Europe and Africa. Just when they arrived in Europe is difficult to say, for there is no record of their entry. We do know that, beginning in A.D. 541 and continuing for about two hundred years, a series of bubonic plague epidemics raged through the Mediterranean area. Presumably it was spread by black rats and their fleas.

No one knows where or when the plague bacilli originated. It probably was either in India or East Africa. By the time of Christ, plague was present in both places. It probably did not reach the steppes of Asia until later—possibly as late as the early 1300s, though it may have arrived earlier, living undetected in wild rodents for some time.

Once plague spreads from wild rodents to rats living in close proximity to human beings, the disease first is transmitted only from rat to rat. When each sick rat dies, its fleas leave the cooling dead body and seek, by preference, warm, living rats on which they might find another comfortable home. Fleas from one dead rat might infest dozens of new rats, thus quickly spreading the disease throughout the rat population. Because the rats soon are dying faster than they reproduce, the rat population decreases in size. From the fleas' point of view, there now is a rat shortage.

Rat fleas then seek other warm bodies. They will accept dogs and cats and some other domestic animals, but they seem to prefer human beings second only to rats. Now the fleas will obtain their food by biting human beings for their blood, and in so doing, may inject plague bacilli into them. Whenever a mass die-off occurs among plague-ridden black rats living close to a human population, there is almost sure to be a plague epidemic among those people.

Plague is most commonly transmitted from rats to human beings by the oriental rat flea (*Xenopsylla cheopsis*). Dog and cat fleas, human fleas, and even lice and

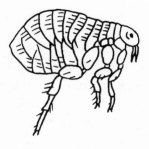

The oriental rat flea.

bedbugs may occasionally do it, but they are rather inefficient.

Fleas feed by biting their hosts and sucking up some of their blood. If a rat flea sucks up blood containing the plague bacilli, the bacilli are taken in along with the blood. Often, the blood and bacilli move smoothly along the flea's digestive system and are digested. In this case, when the flea bites another rat or a human being, there are no plague bacilli in its mouth parts, and the disease is not transmitted to the bitten animal.

In some cases, however, the blood and bacilli form a clot that blocks the flea's digestive system. Such a flea is called a *blocked flea.* Then, when the blocked flea attempts to feed again, its blood meal can move only as far as the clot. The blood is not digested, and the flea gets no nourishment from it. The flea, presumably hungrier than ever, attempts to feed again. As it sucks in more and more blood, some blood along with some of the bacilli is forced back out and is injected into the animal on which the flea is feeding. Only blocked fleas transmit plague bacilli this way, and the oriental rat flea is the insect with the greatest tendency to become blocked.

Once a person is infected, the disease may take any of three forms: *bubonic*, *pneumonic*, and *septicemic*.

Bubonic plague is the most common form. One of the body's means of defense against invading bacteria are *lymph nodes*, which are scattered throughout the body but are most common in the armpits and groin. The lymph nodes act as traps that filter out bacteria in the circulatory system; here the body's white blood cells ordinarily engulf and kill the trapped bacteia. Plague bacilli, however, ordinarily manage to evade the white blood cells and multiply in the lymph nodes, causing them to swell, sometimes to the size of oranges. These swellings, called *buboes*, give bubonic plague its name. Hemorrhages under the skin produce black spots—hence the name Black Death. The disease may run from a few days to a week or more and is characterized by headache, fatigue, chills and fever, nausea, and painful buboes. Without medical treatment, about sixty to ninety percent of people with bubonic plague die. Because there are so few bacilli in the bloodstream, people with bubonic plague rarely transmit it to others.

Pneumonic plague occurs if the plague bacilli reach the lungs and cause pneumonia there. The most infectious form of plague, it is transmitted from human to human directly through the air when bacilli sneezed or coughed up by one person are inhaled by another. No fleas are necessary for the spread of pneumonic plague. In the crowded conditions under which people lived in the Middle Ages, pneumonic plague spread rapidly. Fortunately it was common only in the winter, and it ac-

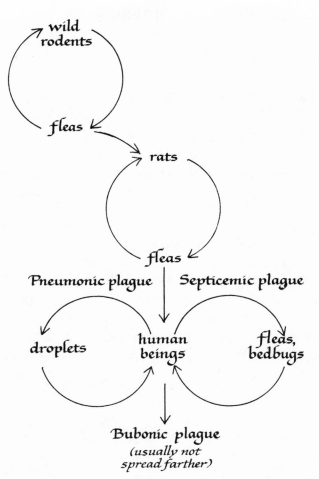

wild
rodents

fleas

rats

fleas

Pneumonic plague | Septicemic plague

droplets

human
beings

fleas,
bedbugs

Bubonic plague
(usually not
spread farther)

The usual cycles by which plague epidemics are spread.
Although individual human beings sometimes get plague
through bites from fleas that move directly from wild
rodents, plague epidemics among human beings are
ordinarily preceded by plague epidemics among black rats
living in houses, barns, or ships. Pneumonic and septicemic
forms of plague may spread from person to person; the
bubonic form rarely is contagious.

counted for only ten to twenty percent of plague deaths during the Black Death. However, it was deadly; once a person had it, there was virtually no chance of recovery. Death usually came within a day after the onset of the first symptoms—hardly time for the dying to put their affairs in order.

Septicemic plague was also fatal. The bacilli reproduced rapidly in the bloodstream, and death came within hours, frequently before any symptoms occurred. The fact that an apparently healthy person could die without warning (some apparently healthy persons went to bed and died in their sleep) must have made the disease even more terrifying. No one knew if he would be alive tomorrow. Because the bloodstream was filled with bacilli, bites of human fleas and bedbugs—which rarely become blocked—could transmit septicemic plague from person to person. Septicemic plague was rare during the Black Death, but it occurred frequently enough to make the epidemic mysterious and frightening.

The Course of the Black Death

THE EPIDEMIC known as the Black Death probably began on the steppes of Mongolia and quickly spread to China about 1330. This was a time when nature seemed to be on a rampage. For several years there had been droughts and earthquakes in China, and they continued through 1333. The next year there was flooding that wiped out some of the crops, and locusts ate up most of the rest. Dislocated from their homes by earthquakes and floods, many of the Chinese people crowded into temporary housing, conditions right for the spread of epidemics. Furthermore, many of the people were starving and therefore more susceptible to disease than usual.

Once the plague had taken hold in China, the bacilli traveled inside the rats, and fleas that accompanied them, along the trade routes. Even without rats, infected fleas can remain alive for long periods of time inside shipments of grain, cloth, or other merchandise. A healthy person might carry infected fleas some distance in his own clothing.

Step by step, through the 1330s and the early 1340s people, animals, trade goods, and the plague moved slowly westward across Asia, each step bringing the plague that much closer to Europe. In 1338–1339, most of the Nestorian Christian community near Lake Issyk Kul in central Asia were killed by the disease. In 1345, it had reached Sarai, north of the Caspian Sea, in western Asia. Later the same year, the Black Death reached the Crimea, a peninsula on the northern shore of the Black Sea. The Black Sea was one of the places where caravans coming from the east met the ships of Mediterranean countries for trading purposes. On the Crimean peninsula was the town of Caffa, where the merchants of Genoa had set up a trading post. From here Genoese ships—often with rats aboard—carried their newly-received goods back to Genoa.

The plague was now in eastern Europe, but it did not proceed much farther into Europe by land, because most of the trade routes continued west by sea. The entry

*The route by which the Black Death crossed Asia in the
1330s and 1340s.*
INSET: Stippling indicates the Crimean Peninsula.

of the Black Death into western Europe was through the
island of Sicily. There, in the harbor of Messina, a Genoese fleet bearing the plague made port in October of 1347.

What no one noticed, or cared about if they did
notice, were the rats that scampered down the ropes securing the ships to the dock. It was a common sight. Of
what importance were a few more rats?

News of the slow westward movement of the Black Death across Asia had been known to the people of Europe for several years. At first most of them felt they had little to worry about. After all, China was so far away. Now the news was that it had reached Constantinople, Alexandria, and Cyprus—all uncomfortably close to them. Then came the day that the citizens of Messina realized that the plague was in their city and that it had probably been brought by the ships in port. They drove out the ships and the sailors, but no one did anything about the rats. By the time the first citizens of the town became ill, fleas from Caffa had settled down among the black rats of Messina.

Soon after the first sickness, hundreds of people died in Messina every day. Panic gripped the city. Because no one saw the connection between rats, fleas, and the sickness, there was no obvious way that the disease spread. (Where anyone thought about the matter at all it was assumed that all those rats dying by the thousands had caught the plague from human beings.) It seemed that just talking to a sick person or even looking at him could make someone ill.

The only thing to do was to leave the city. Many people fled to the countryside. The result was that they spread the disease to other parts of the island. Some went to the nearby city of Catania where there was a hospital. Finally the citizens of Catania realized what had happened and refused to allow more refugees from Messina in. But it was too late. The plague had a firm grip on Catania and soon on all of the island of Sicily.

Merchant ships from Sicily spread the Black Death to southern Italy and also to North Africa. In the meantime, other ships that had touched at ports of the eastern Mediterranean where plague had already taken its toll—Constantinople, Alexandria, and others—were returning home to the great Italian ports especially Genoa and Venice. By the end of the year, plague was raging through these and other Italian cities. In each case the story was much like that of Messina. The city officials recognized too late what the ships had brought, then sent them away carrying the plague to still other ports. In this way the Black Death spread rapidly throughout the Mediterranean.

In January of 1348, the Black Death reached Marseille in France, a few months later it had passed the Strait of Gibraltar and began to work its way up the Atlantic coast of Europe. It was in England by August. In 1349, it reached Ireland and Wales. In 1350, when the epidemic was over in the Mediterranean area, it traveled all the way to Greenland and worked its way across the northern coast of continental Europe, reaching northern Russia by the end of the year.

Wherever the plague entered a port it began to move inland rather rapidly along the trade routes, then slowly but surely to almost every remote village. Great inland cities like Florence and Sienna in Italy, and Paris and Avignon in France were ravaged. Some villages and tiny hamlets were entirely wiped out. Cattle roamed the streets and country lanes unattended, for there was no one to care for them. Buildings of all sorts—houses, barns,

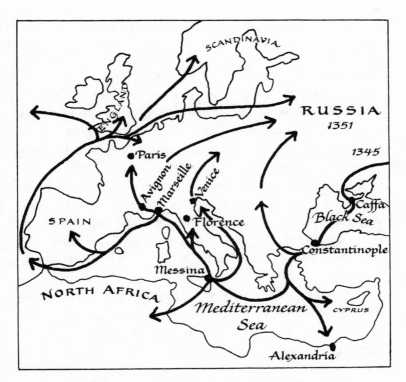

The path of the Black Death through Europe.

mills, churches—were abandoned and fell into disrepair. Where entire families died, there was no one to inherit houses or land. Then a surviving neighbor might take over an abandoned house if he thought it was better than his own; usually there was no one to stop him. (In Scandinavia a little girl inherited an entire town because she was its only survivor.)

Physicians who stayed at their posts died at just as high a rate as their patients. At the University of Mont-

pellier the entire medical staff perished. Other physicians
fled from the cities as the plague arrived. Those who
stayed and survived charged exhorbitant prices. It made
little difference to the people, however, whether physicians died, fled, or continued their practice, for they could
be of little real help. Medicine simply had not advanced
to the point where a physician could know what to do.
One theory that many believed was that the plague was
God's punishment for people's sins, which apparently
were being committed in greater numbers than ever before. A priest might prescribe prayer and repentance for
that, but the wrath of God was beyond the realm of
medicine.

Another theory held that the plague was caused by
hot, foul air presumed to emanate from the ground when
earthquakes or other natural disasters occurred. Some
physicians, therefore, prescribed taking to one's bed and
remaining calm and inactive, for if a person became over-
heated, his pores would open, allowing the bad air to
enter and bring about the disease.

Some physicians prescribed pleasant odors. People
washed their faces with rose-water or vinegar, and they
burned aromatic plants in their rooms. Herbs and spices
were strewn on the floor or were carried in little pouches.
Those physicians who were brave enough actually to visit
patients attempted to protect themselves by covering
their bodies entirely with clothing that included a face
mask with a long beaklike projection in which they carried spices.

*A physician would protect himself
as best he could from the Black Death
while visiting a patient.*

A few physicians were of the opposite opinion. They believed that the only thing that could drive away the foul air was even more foul air. They recommended spending as much time as possible inhaling the stench from latrines. Keeping a bad-smelling billy goat in the house or dead dogs nearby was thought a good preventative.

To draw poisons out of the body some tried totally different remedies such as dried toads or the plucked rear ends of live roosters applied to the buboes.

None of this worked, of course. Sweet- or foul-smelling air, toads or roosters, the fleas still bit.

The only useful advice was to leave the cities early in the hope of finding a place the plague had not reached and would not reach. Unfortunately, people rarely left soon enough. Infected but apparently healthy people arrived in the countryside. Those lucky enough to find places not yet affected were often disappointed that later refugees brought the plague with them.

Almost everyone who could afford to do so left the cities, many in great haste and panic when they heard that the plague was near. Others waited until a member of the family fell ill. Then, in terror that their final days might be near if they waited any longer, they left the sick. Parents deserted children, children deserted parents. Husbands abandoned wives, wives abandoned husbands.

In some places, city officials, hearing that there was plague in a house, boarded up the building leaving all the occupants, ill or well, to perish inside. On the other hand, there were a few cases of wealthy people who, while still in good health, bought a great supply of food and shut themselves up in a house and allowed no one to come in; in a few cases, these people survived. Perhaps they were lucky enough to have rat-free homes.

Food prices soon soared, and food even became impossible to get in some cities because no one would dare to enter a city where the Black Death was present. It was one more reason to seek refuge in the countryside if you could possibly afford to go.

Like the physicians, the church provided little comfort. Perhaps the plague was God's just punishment for an extraordinary amount of sinning. But if that was so, why had not the church warned the people instead of allowing them to fall so deeply into sin? There were few who might even try to answer this question, for most of the clergy, like others, had either fled or were dying of the plague. Although it seems that proportionately more priests stayed at their posts (at least the death rate from plague was higher among priests than among other professionals) than did physicians or lawyers, the fleeing of some priests left a bad impression on the people as a whole who saw it as a failing of the church in general.

In most large cities the plague took eighteen months to two years to run its course. At its peak, it was not unusual for several thousand persons to die each day. In most places there came a day when there were not enough gravediggers to dig individual graves, for not many would take on such a job for any amount of money. Yet, some did. Then carts traveled through the streets day and night to receive corpses that people brought to their front doors. Mass graves were used for these dead and sometimes also for the dying who were too weak to resist their fate. In some cities there were not enough living even to cart the dead away. Piles of corpses left in the streets simply rotted.

Graveyards filled rapidly. New ones had to be dug. This created a problem for Catholics—and with the exception of the Jewish community and some Moslems in the south—nearly all Europeans were Catholic then. It was important for them to be buried in consecrated ground, and it was not always possible to have the new graveyards consecrated in time—partly because the corpses accumulated so fast, and partly because many clergymen, like other citizens, had fled from the cities. In Avignon, where the plague hit about as fiercely as in any other major city, Pope Clement VI consecrated the Rhone River so that bodies could be dumped directly into it. This may have improved the situation in Avignon, but the coming of thousands of diseased bodies could hardly have been welcomed by the people living downstream.

Another concern of Catholics is to be able to confess their sins to a priest when death seems near but there were not enough priests to hear deathbed confessions. In 1349, an English bishop issued a decree that in the absence of a priest, a dying person might confess his sins to any man or—in what must reflect the desperateness of the situation—to a woman if a man could not be found.

The Effect of the Black Death on Society

UNDER THE TERRIBLE PRESSURES of seeing so many of their relatives and friends sicken and die, not knowing if they themselves would be next, and having no sure, safe place to go, people reacted in different ways. Some became pious and religious, devoting what might be their last days on earth to prayer; they gave generous gifts outright to the church or left them in their wills. Others sought to enjoy to the utmost whatever time might be left to them and indulged themselves in whatever pleasures they chose. Many stole from the dead or dying and looted abandoned houses.

One response of people who are trapped in an unpleasant situation from which there is no escape is to put the blame on someone else—especially on a minority group. Beginning in 1348, when the Black Death had taken a firm hold on Europe, Christians in several places, but especially in Swiss and German towns, put the blame on the Jewish population. The plague, they claimed, had been caused by the poisoning of wells by Jews who supposedly then got their drinking water elsewhere. Jews were also accused of obtaining the pus from buboes of plague victims and spreading it on the houses of Christians. No one seemed to notice that Jews were dying of the plague just as Christians were. In several towns, including Chillon, Basel, Bern, and Freiburg, Jews were tortured horribly and forced to confess that not only they themselves, but their relatives and Jewish acquaintances, had spread the plague. All Jews implicated in this way— which meant the entire Jewish population in some towns—were then executed, usually in some terrible way such as burning to death. Thousands perished this way.

Although Pope Clement VI declared the Jews to be innocent of such crimes, the people continued the persecutions. As a result, many Jews fled eastward into Poland and Russia, where the local populations were more tolerant—perhaps because the plague had not yet reached there.

At the same time, there were other people who put the blame for the Black Death squarely on their own sins. They punished themselves by whipping themselves—an act called *flagellism*. Flagellism was not a new phenomenon among Christians, but with the coming of the Black Death, a cult of flagellants sprang up. The practice was especially popular in Germany. Arranging themselves in long processions, flagellants marched from town to town. They carried knotted whips with small, sharp pieces of iron held in the knots. At each town they would perform public ceremonies in which they whipped themselves until their blood flowed.

These ceremonies were believed to prevent plague and even to cure it. Flagellants came to be considered almost holy persons, and the sick or their relatives welcomed them into their homes. People sought to obtain just a drop of blood from their bleeding backs. Unfortunately, the flagellants had no power to cure or even prevent plague. Worse, their marchings through the countryside undoubtedly helped to spread it. The first flagellants probably were sincere, but they were later joined by criminals. Townspeople no longer welcomed them, and the cult died out.

No one knows exactly how many people died in the Black Death. Only a few of the survivors recorded their impressions of the devastation, and the numbers of dead that some of them gave exceeded the entire population of the city or town in which they lived. In the case of large cities, such figures must be exaggerations, but it is possible that in small towns, to which many city-dwellers fled, the total number of dead might have exceeded the permanent population.

Very few towns kept accurate official records of deaths. Even if it was the custom of a city to keep records, the number grew too fast for an accurate counting. Then, too, the recorders of such information died or disappeared at a fast rate just like everyone else. The Catholic church, however, did keep records of the number of clergymen who had to be replaced. Largely on the basis of this, it is estimated that out of a total population of 75 million persons, 25 million Europeans died in the four years that it took the plague to run through western Europe. One out of every three persons had died. Many cities lost forty to fifty percent of their populations or even more. A few remote towns were lucky, and the plague never reached them; others were wiped out completely. Today in Europe there are remains of thousands of abandoned villages, some so nearly totally destroyed that they were discovered only recently by outlines in aerial photographs that mark where walls or fences once stood.

After the Black Death

WHEN THE BLACK DEATH had run its course in Europe, the survivors had only about ten years to bring their lives back in order when a second epidemic of plague struck, this one almost as bad as the first. It killed about a fifth to a fourth of the people. This epidemic took proportionately more of the children than had the Black Death. In so doing it took away many of the people who might have had babies in another ten or twenty years thus forestalling for a longer time a return to normal population growth. A few years later a third epidemic came which, in turn, was not quite so bad as the second. For more than 300 years plague epidemics recurred at intervals of about five to twenty years. With some exceptions each one was generally less severe than the one preceding it. Generally, too, later epidemics affected smaller areas than earlier ones had.

As a consequence of this the population of Europe, which in 1347 had been the highest it had ever been, declined steadily until about fifty years after the Black Death, when it began to rise again. It was another 100 years (about 1500) before Europe's population returned to the level that existed before the onset of the Black Death.

The effect of all this dying went beyond simple fluctuations in population size. The daily lives of people changed. One of the immediate effects was that of disruption of services that everyone had taken for granted before the Black Death. We have seen that there were not enough gravediggers to bury all the dead. The survivors had to put up with the stench of rotting corpses in neighboring houses or in the streets, but that soon came to an end.

In towns deserted by physicians, the people had to manage without the comfort of medical care. Thus, the Black Death caused people to lose faith in medicine. Physicians had been able to offer no more useful suggestions than to run away. After the Black Death, medical men began to take another look at their profession. Instead of following blindly the old superstitions, they began, slowly at first, methods of experimental research. Hospitals, which had previously been places where only the dying entered in desperation, became cleaner institutions where there was some hope of cure. It was a while before many practical results were achieved, but, by about 1500, physicians had started on the long path to modern medicine.

The Black Death also caused some people to lose faith in their religion at just the time when they felt the greatest need for spiritual comfort. It must have been bad enough to live through the first epidemic and see all that dying, but to experience repeated epidemics and to expect more to come must have been psychologically shattering. With nowhere else to look for comfort, many decided that rather than following an organized church they would find their own private way to God. Some undertook pilgrimages to holy places; during later epidemics this helped to spread the plague again. Others depended on earning salvation by the giving of large gifts to the church, which grew rich on charity. These attitudes and subsequent allegations of corruption laid the groundwork for several attempts to reform the Catholic church. In the 1500s the great Protestant Reformation split the church. After that there were years of religious wars and persecutions, but they led eventually in many countries to the freedom to choose one's own religion—or to choose to have none at all.

As the number of dead rose during the Black Death, so did the numer of wills that had to be probated, but the number of lawyers available to do the job had decreased. Survivors had to wait a long time for inheritances to be settled. When the inheritances were finally straightened out, a lot of the survivors were better off than before. If the property of the one-third of the population who died went to the two-thirds who survived, the survivors, on the average, were fifty percent richer than they had been before. Most of the property, of course, had been in the hands of the rich, and most of it passed down to their relatives. In the cities, this created huge fortunes for the already wealthy, but, oddly enough, in the countryside, it turned out to be unexpectedly advantageous for the poor serfs.

The lord of a manor, as we have seen in the first chapter, relied on the labor of the serfs to work his land. When the lord inherited more land, as most of the surviving lords did, he needed more serfs to do the work if all that land was to be productive and to be put to crops. But the Black Death had reduced the number of serfs. In fact, proportionately more of the serfs died than did the lords, because most serfs could not afford to flee from the plague whereas most of the lords did. On the average, a lord might now have almost fifty percent more land to work but at least thirty-three percent fewer workers to care for it (on some manors *all* the serfs had died). Furthermore, it was customary for a serf who had inherited something to pay a sort of inheritance tax to his lord. Usually the tax was not in the form of money, but an animal—a horse or a cow, for instance. When the surviving serfs paid their taxes, many lords of manors found themselves owning more animals than ever before, and so they needed even more workers.

The serfs saw that they, who had once been nothing but cheap labor because there were so many of them, were now in short supply. They demanded more compensation for their work, and they often demanded it in cash. Instead of receiving rent in exchange for labor, they received cash, and they paid cash for rent. What was left over they might save or spend on a few luxuries. In the earlier barter system there was nothing that could be saved. Now, if a lord did not give in to his serfs' demands, they would seek employment from other lords who were happy to pay the higher wages rather than lose their crops.

This was another important factor in the breaking up of the feudal system, which was already beginning to disintegrate. The peasants were no longer bound to the land or to a particular lord. They were, in effect, no longer serfs. They could walk away from the manor on which they had been born and earn cash for their labors almost anywhere they pleased. The lords, in turn, saw that the manor system was no longer profitable. Many of them gave it up and rented out their lands for cash. Where sheep could be raised, some of them converted their manors to sheep pastures. Sheep gave two salable commodities—wool and meat—and required only a few shepherds and dogs to guard them.

The common man thus became more independent in his choice of occupation. Not only was he no longer bound to a particular lord, he no longer had to farm for a living. He could follow whatever occupation suited him. Some serfs went to the cities to try their luck as craftsmen, also in short supply.

Once people received cash wages, time acquired a new value. A person worked so many hours for so much money. Clocks, which had formerly been used almost exclusively in monasteries to determine the hours for prayers, now timed the work day as well. If time was worth money, employers wanted that time to be used most productively. Labor-saving (therefore, time-saving) devices came to be invented and used more frequently than before. Improvements were made in windmills, water wheels, and construction of ships. The printing press was a labor-saving device for book manufacturing, but it had a more far-reaching effect—it brought information and knowledge to people who would never have had the money to buy an expensive handwritten book.

The difficulty of keeping peasants bound to the land and the consequent difficulty of managing the lands were part of the cause of the downfall of the feudal system. As we saw in the last chapter, another was the developing use of gunpowder on the battlefield, which took away the knights' reason for existence. By 1500, the feudal system was on its way out in parts of Europe, especially western Europe.

With a reduced population after the Black Death, Europe of the late 1300s needed less land for agriculture. Marginal lands, the lands less suitable for cultivation but which had been put into production since the late 1200s only because there were so many people, were taken out of production after the Black Death. This allowed the soil to recover some of its fertility and forests to return in some places. But by 1500, Europe's population was about where it had been when the Black Death first struck, and Europe was about to run out of good farming land again.

While many nobles lost their fortunes, other people, some previously poor, were suddenly making a great deal of money. The newly rich, having lived through one or more epidemics of plague and not knowing when it might return again and take them, used their new wealth to buy expensive and showy clothes, jewels, and furs. They wanted luxury items, not only those that were manufactured in Europe, but more exotic ones such as silks and gems from the Far East and furs that came now only from the forests of Scandinavia or the more distant Siberia. Merchants, who were part of the growing middle class, looked for markets for the products of their industries. This double desire for trade—buying of exotic items and selling of European products—led to the search for new trade routes. One such search led to the unexpected finding of North and South America, two continents previously unknown to Europe. That happened in 1492, just in time for these new and sparsely populated lands to begin to absorb some of the growing population of Europe.

This was a population with a different outlook on life from that of their ancestors who lived before or during the Black Death. These were people free to come and go more or less as they pleased. They were willing to take their chances on exploring the unknown regions of the world, pay for their own mistakes, and profit from their own discoveries without being dependent on the protection of a lord. Although many failed and some died in adventurous explorations, there was always the expectation of profits for the brave and daring. It was an age, too, of inventions. Men sailed on ships that were being improved continually and were guided by new and better instruments. The information that they brought back was printed on the new printing presses and so made available to anyone who cared to read about it.

With these changes in society, the Middle Ages came to an end, and the modern world began. The Reformation, the discovery of America, and inventions like the printing press would certainly have occurred eventually. But the rats and fleas that brought all the horrors and terrors of the Black Death also pushed us into the modern world a little sooner.

CHAPTER 3

Beaver and the Exploration of Canada

WE ARE PECULIAR among mammals in having bodies with such a scant covering of hair. Therefore, it is hardly a wonder that throughout our history, people have used the furry skins of slain animals to keep themselves warm. In some climates fur is an absolute necessity to protect the human body from cold; in some others, a comfortable convenience.

What is not a necessity is the wearing of fur as an ornament, yet long ago fur became fashionable the world over. Even in warm climates, where fur can be uncomfortable to wear, people who can afford to buy it often show off that fact by wearing it. It is largely fashion that has driven some fur-bearing animals to the brink of extinction—or over it—in some parts of the world. In earlier times it was fashion that drove hunters and trappers farther and farther into some unexplored areas to seek fresh hunting grounds.

Furs in the Middle Ages

DURING MOST of the Middle Ages poverty kept most people who were serfs from wearing furs. Only royalty, nobility, and the very rich could afford to buy fur. In fact, laws were sometimes passed which forbade the common people to wear furs and prescribed what furs people of different social rank were permitted to wear. Furs became a symbol of the wearer's social standing—a true status symbol. In 1294, for instance, only ladies of the French nobility were permitted to wear ermine-lined dresses.

Near the end of the Middle Ages, some of the growing middle class—merchants, bankers, and lawyers, for instance—were beginning to make more money than ever before. The laws about who could wear what furs were ignored more and more. People bought and wore whatever they wanted and could afford. With only the thought of profit in their minds, hunters killed off animals faster than they could reproduce. As a consequence, many species of fur-bearing animals began to disappear in large areas of Europe.

This was especially true of the European beaver (*Castor fiber*; the American beaver is *Castor canadensis*). Its near demise in Europe came about because of a fashion that started in the 1300s and continued for several hundred years—the beaver hat. Beaver skins had long been used for warm clothing, but hats made of sheared beaver (beaver skins with the fur trimmed short) now came into

Beaver.

style. Then, about 1600, someone discovered that beaver fur made excellent felt. The individual hairs have small, microscopic barbs. When the hairs are cut from the fur and matted down, the barbs allow the individual hairs to become caught on each other, producing a strong material. Hats of beaver felt now became all the rage. By this time beavers had become extinct in most parts of Europe and nearly so in Scandinavia. Many other fur-bearing animals were becoming rare there, too.

As a result hunters of furs shifted their activities eastward into Asia, where the great forests of Siberia stretched for thousands of miles to the Pacific Ocean. These forests, too, had once contained plenty of beaver and other fur bearers, but as the animal populations were decimated in western Asia, hunters had to move still farther eastward. It became ever more costly to transport furs across Asia to Europe. Furs were an expensive luxury, but one that almost everyone wanted.

In 1492, Christopher Columbus, with the financial backing of King Ferdinand and Queen Isabella of Spain had sailed to the west looking for a short route to Asia. What he found instead were entirely new lands, which he thought at first to be islands off the coast of Asia. Spain, which claimed as its own all the territory he found, intended to take as much more of the still unexplored lands as it could.

After several years, expeditions from Spain and France had explored enough of the eastern coasts of the newly discovered lands to make it certain that Columbus had not reached any place near Asia. There were two large continents—soon to be called North America and South America—blocking the way.

The French Come to North America

IN 1534, King Francis I of France commissioned sea captain Jacques Cartier to search for a passage—later to be known as the Northwest Passage—whereby ships might sail through or around North America to Asia. In the summer of that year, Cartier crossed the Atlantic and found the mouth of a large river. The following year, on a second expedition, he returned to explore this great river. On these trips he found that the people living there—the Micmac and Huron Indians—had beaver robes and other furs that they were willing to trade for manufactured European goods.

At one village, in what was apparently a misunderstanding, Cartier asked in sign language, "What is the name of this place?" The Indians, thinking he had asked what they called their huts, replied, "Kanata." With a slight change of spelling the village was labeled Canada on early French maps of the area. Cartier called the great river on which it stood the River of Canada; now it is the St. Lawrence River. The land on either side of the river soon was called Canada and, later, New France.

Proceeding upstream in the hope that the river would lead him to the western sea and so to Asia, Cartier was eventually stopped by tremendous rapids near what is now the city of Montreal. The French later called that rapids La Chine (now Lachine), the French name for China. It reflected the hope of Cartier and some who followed him that China would not be far beyond. It was

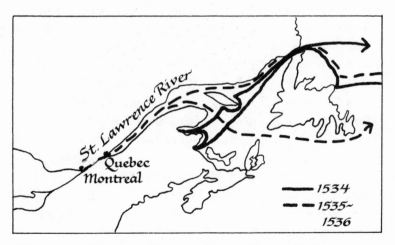

The routes of Jacques Cartier's first and second trips to North America.

the kind of mistake people would continue to make for more than 250 years.

The Huron Indians living there had told Cartier of great seas that lay to the west, but these were in the territory of hostile Iroquois tribes, and he was not encouraged to explore in that direction. After spending an amazingly cold winters for natives of France—their ships were frozen into their harbor and twenty-five men died of scurvy or cold—the remainder of Cartier's expedition returned to France in 1536. Though they had not reached Asia, they had explored farther into the North American continent than any Europeans before them.

By the accepted rules among European nations then, a country could claim as its possessions any lands that had been discovered and explored by its own people provided those lands were not already the possession of another Christian nation. The lands to be possessed did not have to be extensively explored. It was sufficient to explore partway up a river to have a legitimate claim to all the land drained by all the tributaries of that river. Thus Cartier's trip up the St. Lawrence River as far as Montreal gave France a legitimate claim to all the land drained by the Great Lakes, which no white man had seen and only vaguely knew existed at that time. Except for the Spanish conquest of Mexico far to the south, no other European power was yet laying serious claim to any other part of North America. Therefore, by some extension of its proper claim, France simply claimed all of North America north of Mexico even though no one had any idea how much land or how many other river systems it might contain. Neither did anyone have the remotest idea then of what a treasury it was in furs alone.

To lay claim to North America was one thing; to retain the land claimed was another. A country really had to establish permanent settlements and to provide them with armed forces to protect them—from both the original inhabitants of the land who were likely to resent the intrusion and from some other (probably European) power that wanted it also. France attempted to establish settlements on the St. Lawrence River between 1541 and 1543, but they failed. The resistance of the Huron Indians, who had been happy to trade but not to see the French settle in their lands, and the bitter winters during which many of the settlers perished from cold or scurvy discouraged those who survived the attempt. They returned to France.

It was not until the early 1600s that the French made another, and, this time, successful attempt to settle in North America. By this time, hats of beaver felt were in high fashion. And there, in the continent that France claimed as its possession, were millions of beaver just for the taking.

Beaver are aquatic mammals living in relatively small, gently flowing streams. With the trees the beaver cut down, they dam streams, forming quiet ponds in which they build—also from downed trees—their homes, called *lodges*. The lodges extend above the water but have underwater entrances through which the beaver can come and go with relative safety from most predators.

The northern part of North America—roughly what

are Canada and Alaska today—was once covered by great glaciers. The action of these glaciers gouged out of the land not only the five Great Lakes, but thousands of lakes, ranging from a few larger than the smallest of the Great Lakes, to tiny ponds too small and too many even to be given names. Like beads on necklaces they are connected by great rivers and tiny rivulets. Nowhere else in the world is there so vast a land covered with such a dense

The distribution of beaver (black and stippling) in North America, and the distribution of aspen trees (black). Because the aspen is the beaver's favorite tree for food and for building dams and lodges, the black area on the map is the best beaver country. Because this northern area has cold winters, it is also where beavers grow the thickest and most desired fur.

network of waterways. Northern North America contains more than half of all the fresh water in the world, and a great deal of the land is forested. Although the natural home of the American beaver includes nearly all of North America, the northern wooded areas provide plenty of aspen trees, which beavers prefer in building their dams and homes, and from which they obtain the bark they eat. Here, where the winters are among the coldest in the world, beavers grow thick, luxuriant fur. Northern North America, therefore, provided everything necessary for the maintenance of a large beaver population with the most desirable fur. France had claimed the best beaver country in the world just as the demand for beaver fur was at a peak.

In 1605, Samuel Champlain, after several failures, established the first permanent French settlement of Port Royal in New France. In 1608, he founded a trading post—mostly for furs—near where Quebec City stands today, and shortly thereafter another at the site of Montreal, which later would become the major fur-trading city of Canada.

Permanent trading with the Indians began with the Hurons who occupied the region north of the St. Lawrence River and the eastern Great Lakes. Over nearly three centuries the trade would gradually spread to almost every tribe that lived in what is now modern Canada and in much of what is now the United States.

In the fur trade the French did some hunting, but most of them functioned as traders. It was the Indians who hunted and trapped and brought the furs to the trading posts. The French in the trading posts received from France shipments of manufactured goods, mostly items of steel or wool. The Huron Indians had almost no metal technology, and metal items made their lives much easier. Knives and axes that did not have to be laboriously chipped from stone were a great convenience. So were needles that did not have to be made from bone. Woolen clothing dried much faster after becoming wet than did the traditional animal skins that the Indians wore.

While this trade made Indians' lives easier, over the years it also made some of them lose part of their own culture as they forgot old skills. They became dependent on the French (and later the English) to supply them with items they could not manufacture themselves. The French, in turn, were dependent on the Indians to supply furs and sometimes food—which may have been shot with European guns and ammunition. French industry, just having come out of the Middle Ages, was given a boost by this new market for their manufactured goods. At one time they even manufactured metal arrowheads to Indian specifications.

Under this fur-trading system, in which the two peoples found a mutual dependence on each other, relationships with the Indians were usually far better than they were between Indians and agricultural settlers elsewhere. A farmer needs land, and farmers had the tendency, at the very least, to take land away from the Indians, and at the worst to kill them to prevent their trying to get their land back. In the fur trade, however, the Indians were essential to the successful pursuit of the business. They were the ones who actually did the work of obtaining the furs. The French fur traders and the Indian hunters and trappers, therefore, got along rather well. (The French did find themselves in uncomfortable situations, though, when caught up in intertribal warfare, some of which centered on what tribes were going to control hunting territories.)

So great was the French demand for furs that soon the fur-bearing animals—and most especially the beaver—had been annihilated in the area immediately around the St. Lawrence River. Axes, guns, and plenty of ammunition made it much easier for Indians to kill animals.

When hunting became poor in their area, the Huron Indians living immediately around the French settlements converted to become traders themselves. As neighboring tribes to the north and west—the Montagnais, the Algonquins, and the Ottawas—saw European products, they, too, wanted them, and to get them they traded furs with the Hurons who, in turn, traded them to the French. After a while, furs were coming to the St. Lawrence area from a long distance away—far enough that several French traders thought it worth their while to travel into the forests themselves. This way they could eliminate the Indian middleman and take that much more profit for themselves. These enterprising Frenchmen carried manufactured goods with them and traded them directly with the more distant Indian tribes. At first the trader might be gone from his home for a few days, then, when beaver gradually became scarce in the new area, for a few weeks, over the winter, and eventually for a year or two. Thus began the profession known in the French fur trade as *coureur de bois* (French for "runner of the woods").

Although the name might suggest that the coureurs de bois traveled on foot, they actually made their way almost exclusively by water. In a country without roads but with so many waterways, the best way to travel was in birch-bark canoes, which the Indians taught the white men to make. Canoes skimmed much more easily along the water than did the wooden longboats to which Europeans had been accustomed.

By canoe, coureurs de bois explored the tributaries of the St. Lawrence River. One of these tributaries was the Ottawa, which enters the St. Lawrence just below the Lachine Rapids. In 1615, Champlain went up the Ottawa River, then by way of one of its tributaries to Lake Nipissing, and from there down the French River to a huge "sea" of which the Indians had told him. In addition to exploring fur country, Champlain was looking for the western sea, the long desired route to Asia. Disappointingly, this sea's waters were fresh, not salty. Champlain had come upon Lake Huron, the first of the five Great Lakes to be discovered by a white man. After that, it was only a matter of time before the French discovered the other four. In fact, Champlain saw Lake Ontario on his return trip.

As years went by, it became necessary to travel farther and farther to reach beaver country. It also became necessary to bring back more furs in each trip to make the long trip worthwhile and, of course, that meant

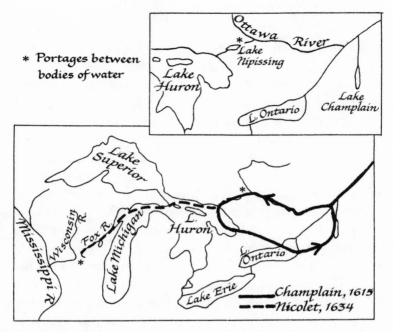

The routes of Champlain's and Nicolet's explorations in the Great Lakes area.

carrying more trade goods in order to obtain that much beaver. What was needed was a large canoe, too large for one man to handle alone. And so came into being another professional, the canoeman known as a *voyageur*.

Paddling the canoes were six to eight voyageurs. They did most of the hard work, paddling in unison with only short breaks during most of the sunlit hours of the day. Where rapids or waterfalls made the streams dangerous or impassable, voyageurs unloaded the canoes and carried them and their contents separately around the rapids in as many trips as necessary. A detour around a rapids was called a *portage* (from the French word *porter*, "to carry"). A portage might also be made between nearby lakes or rivers not connected to each other. A portage might be only a few steps long or a few miles. Grand Portage on the north shore of Lake Superior was named for its nine-mile portage.

Trade goods and furs were packed in bundles of uniform weight: ninety pounds. Each voyageur was expected to carry two packages at a time, but to save time, many voyageurs carried more. A canoe, depending on its size, might hold a cargo of up to five tons. All this hard work was done by voyageurs who usually were not more than five feet, two inches tall. Larger men were not wanted because they took up too much precious space in the canoes.

In 1634, Jean Nicolet, another Frenchman looking for a passage through the continent, became the first white man to travel from Lake Huron into Lake Michigan. Keeping to its westward shore in the hope of discovering the route to Asia, Nicolet found only a dead end—Green Bay. The Fox River, which drained into it, was too small to be a significant route to Asia.

The Indians told Nicolet of a "Big Water" that lay only three days' journey to the west. It must, he reasoned, be the western ocean. Oddly enough, he never took the few extra days to check it out.

The English Come to Hudson Bay

WHILE THE FRENCH explored the Great Lakes, other countries had been taking an interest in finding the hoped-for Northwest Passage. In 1609, Henry Hudson, sailing for the Dutch, discovered instead the Hudson River, thereby giving the Dutch a claim on that river.

The next year, Henry Hudson, now sailing for the English, once more sought the Northwest Passage, this time to the north of the continent. He found a huge bay, which, at first, he thought might be the Pacific Ocean, but it turned out to be another dead end. There he perished when his mutinous crew set him, his son, and several others adrift in a small boat.

Hudson Bay, named in his honor, was a disappointment to the English, too, and they forgot for a while about exploration in its dangerously cold, iceberg-strewn water. Instead, they concentrated on establishing colonies on the more hospitable coasts south of the St. Lawrence River.

By the 1650s, however, coureurs de bois had been going as far west as the area around Michilimackinac and Sault Ste. Marie (the area where Lakes Huron, Michigan, and Superior meet). Among these men were two brothers-in-law named Pierre Esprit Radisson and Médart Chouart, Sieur des Groseilliers. (If you have difficulty with Groseilliers' name, you might think of him as Mr. Gooseberry—a good translation of his name and exactly what the English with whom he later dealt called him.) On one of their trips (1658–1660), they wintered on the north shore of Lake Superior. Here they acquired sixty canoeloads of prime beaver pelts. Here they also learned from the Indians that only a short distance from Lake Superior the rivers all ran north and emptied into a large sea. These rivers, they knew, were where the best beaver furs were now coming from, and they guessed correctly that the sea into which the rivers emptied was Hudson Bay.

In 1660, Radisson and Groseilliers returned to Montreal with their sixty canoes. They had brought back a fortune in beaver. Unfortunately, they had gone into the wilderness without obtaining a required permit to do so, and to their shocked amazement, the governor of New France fined them. He confiscated more than half of the beaver pelts and could not be persuaded to return them. Angry, Radisson and Groseilliers sailed to France in the hope of getting financial backing for a scheme they had devised to control the best beaver country known to exist. That scheme was to sail directly into Hudson Bay, which penetrated the very heart of that country.

No one in France would have any part of the scheme, and so, still angry over their loss, the two brothers-in-law went to England. There, Radisson married a woman whose father introduced him to Prince Rupert, a cousin of King Charles II. High-living Prince Rupert, usually in need of money, was interested in their idea. After all, England had a claim on the Hudson Bay area by virtue of Henry Hudson's explorations there.

Soon Radisson and Groseilliers, financed by Prince Rupert, set out in two ships for Hudson Bay. Radisson's ship had to turn back, but Groseilliers reached James Bay, the southerly extension of Hudson Bay. Here he built Fort Charles at the mouth of the Rupert River. The next year he returned to England with beaver pelts worth thirty times the cost of the goods traded for them.

Spurred on by this easy success, Prince Rupert and several of his friends formed what came to be called the Hudson's Bay Company. In 1670, King Charles granted a royal charter to the company. It was certainly one of the most generous grants ever made; it gave the Hudson's Bay Company title to all the land that drained into Hudson Bay. Called Rupert's Land, it was to be administered by the Hudson's Bay Company, which acted, in effect, as the government of what amounted to an English colony, and Prince Rupert was appointed the first governor of the company.

King Charles had no way of knowing how generous he had been to his cousin. Hardly any white men had set foot in the Hudson Bay drainage area, and no one knew how extensive it was. King Charles had just given to the Hudson's Bay Company 1.5 million square miles of land—nearly one sixth of North America—and, at the same time, the French believed it belonged to them.

The Hudson's Bay Company quickly set up new trading posts on James Bay: Moose Fort at the mouth of the Moose River and Fort Albany at the mouth of the Albany River. These two rivers and Rupert River and their tributaries fanned out from the southern end of James Bay and commanded most of the land between it and the Great Lakes. In 1682, farther to the north, the Hudson's Bay Company built Fort Nelson (later York Factory) where the Nelson and Hayes Rivers empty into Hudson Bay. In 1688, still farther north, they built Prince of Wales Fort (later Fort Churchill) at the mouth of the Churchill River. Into these three rivers flowed waters

According to the grant given to Hudson's Bay Company by King Charles II, Rupert's Land was to include the entire drainage system of Hudson Bay (black).

that passed through nearly all the remaining good beaver country in Rupert's Land. The Hudson's Bay Company could, in theory, at least, expect beaver pelts to come in from nearly as far south as Lake Superior and as far west as the Rocky Mountains (though no one in the company had yet seen the Rocky Mountains).

Ships, of course, had to arrive and leave in July or August. At other times ice was likely to block the way. A late departure from James Bay meant a ship would be frozen in until next spring. Yet, the Hudson's Bay Company had two great advantages over the French traders. The French now had to travel a long and arduous way by canoe along routes that had many portages in order to get to the western Great Lakes country. The English, on the other hand, could disembark from their ships directly into the heart of beaver country. In fact, the English fur traders did not develop the habit of going out and living among the Indians as the coureurs de bois did. They stayed at their fortified trading posts and let the Indians bring their furs to them. In addition, English trade goods

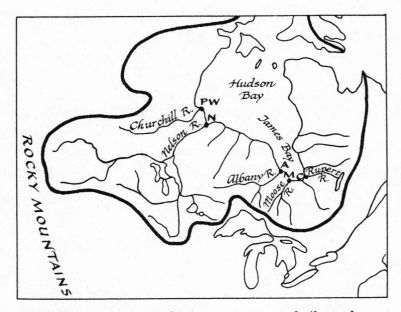

The early Hudson's Bay Company posts were built on the shores of Hudson Bay, but they commanded the rivers that drained large areas of the best beaver country in Rupert's Land. PW—Prince of Wales Fort. N—Fort Nelson. A—Fort Albany. M—Moose Fort. C—Fort Charles.

cost less to make than the French goods did, and therefore the English could afford to give a little more in exchange for furs of equal value than the French did. For this reason Indians were willing to travel greater distances to trade with the English. It was not long before the French fur trade felt the effect of competition from the English. More of the best furs were now being diverted north to Hudson Bay.

The French Gain, the French Lose

DRIVEN BY THE PRESENCE of the English both to the north and along the Atlantic seaboard, New France sought to control more land by continuing explorations to the south and the west. The French knew by now that the "Big Water" of which Nicolet had been told was no ocean but the Mississippi River. There was some hope, however, that the Mississippi River drained into the Gulf of California, which the Spanish had discovered to the southwest. If so, the French would be on the verge of discovering the passage to Asia.

The explorations of Marquette and Joliet and of La Salle along the Mississippi River.
UPPER INSET: With only the upper portion of the Mississippi River explored, the French hoped that the river would flow westward and empty into the Gulf of California and therefore into the Pacific Ocean.
INSET TO RIGHT: Two portages between the Great Lakes and Mississippi systems. The small river flowing into Lake Michigan is the southern branch of the Chicago River.

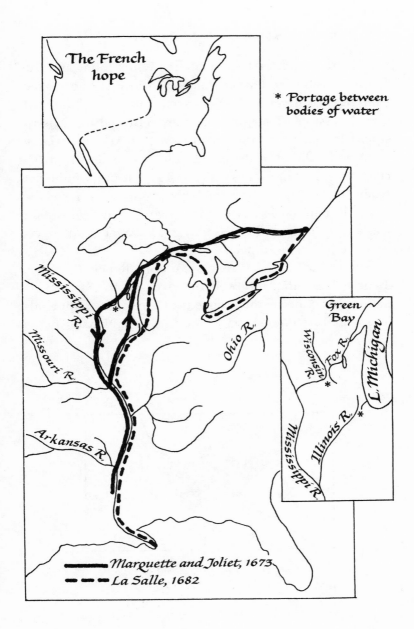

The French
hope

* Portage between
bodies of water

Mississippi R.

Missouri R.

Arkansas R.

Ohio R.

Green
Bay

Wisconsin R.

Fox R.

Illinois R.

L. Michigan

Mississippi R.

———— Marquette and Joliet, 1673
- - - - La Salle, 1682

To that end, in 1673, explorer Louis Joliet and the Jesuit missionary Father Jacques Marquette portaged from the Fox River to the Wisconsin River, a tributary of the Mississippi. That summer they followed the Mississippi River as far as the present state of Arkansas. They went no farther, for at this point it was obvious that the river was flowing almost directly south and would not reach the Gulf of California. They were aware from the size of its tributaries that the Mississippi drainage system was a large one—and it was also good beaver country, especially its northern part.

In 1682, another French explorer, Robert Cavelier, Sieur de La Salle, followed the river all the way to its mouth and claimed for France the entire Mississippi valley, which he named Louisiana in honor of King Louis XIV of France.

The Mississippi drainage area (black) was claimed by France and called Louisiana.

The French decided also to move up into Rupert's Land to recover lost trade with the Indians. In March of 1686, with the northern winter still gripping the land, Captain Pierre de Troyes left Lachine to travel overland by canoe (but with much portaging because many of the streams they followed were frozen) to lead an attack on the Hudson's Bay Company forts on James Bay. Up until then no white men had approached the bay from this direction in the winter. The English expected no hostile force to travel so far in such weather and were taken by surprise. Moose Fort, Fort Rupert (formerly Fort Charles), and Fort Albany fell in rapid succession to the French.

From the Gulf of Mexico to James Bay and from the mouth of the St. Lawrence River to the western end of Lake Superior, the French occupied a great swath that cut through the continent from north to south and half-way across it from east to west. But New France did not yet occupy all of North America.

Therefore, beyond the Great Lakes, to the north-west, the French continued to expand into Rupert's Land. There were no English there to stop them. The English were still clinging to their few remaining posts on Hud-son Bay. The French expansion into Rupert's Land was done partly to cut off the flow of as much beaver to the Hudson's Bay Company as possible, and partly to reach the western sea before the English did. The French were now sure that the Pacific Ocean lay only a short distance beyond Lake Superior.

Coureurs de bois coming from Montreal usually

The lands (black) actually occupied
by the French during the early 1700s.

stopped at Grand Portage on the north shore of Lake Superior. Near there the Pigeon River and a series of small lakes now form the border between the state of Minnesota in the United States and the province of Ontario in Canada. From the mouth of the Pigeon River it is only about fifty miles (as the crow flies) to the divide that separates the Lake Superior drainage from the Hudson Bay drainage. From there, the coureurs de bois gradually extended the fur trade westward and northwestward. They established trading posts at Rainy Lake, then Lake of the Woods, then Lakes Winnipeg and Winnipegosis, and along the Saskatchewan River deep into the heart of the great Canadian prairies—probably to within sight of the Canadian Rocky Mountains. It was the French and not the English who were exploring Rupert's Land. As

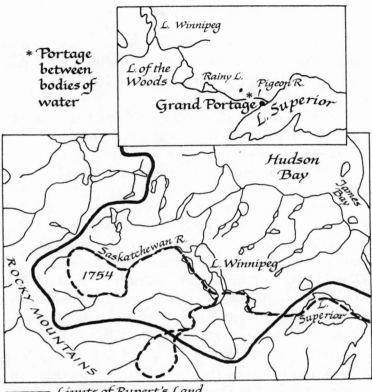

* Portage between bodies of water

L. Winnipeg

L. of the Woods

Rainy L.

Pigeon R.

Grand Portage

L. Superior

Hudson Bay

James Bay

Saskatchewan R.

1754

L. Winnipeg

ROCKY MOUNTAINS

L. Superior

━━━ Limits of Rupert's Land
━ ━ ━ French explorations west of Lake Superior

The westernmost French explorations did not quite reach the Rocky Mountains.
INSET: One of the portages between the Great Lakes and Rupert's Land. This one was used for many years as a route to western Rupert's Land.

usual in the fur trade, they decimated the population of fur-bearing animals as they went, taking the profits, moving on, and leaving behind a place of less value to the fur trade.

The French might have gone even farther west—crossing the Rocky Mountains and reaching the Pacific Ocean—had it not been for the trouble being caused by the competition between France and England for possession of beaver lands.

The tension between the French and the English ended in a series of four wars known collectively in America as the French and Indian Wars (battles were also fought in Europe, where the wars had different names). They lasted, off and on, from 1689 to 1763. In North America each side was aided by those Indian tribes who thought that their best interests lay with one side or the other.

In the end, the French lost, and they lost all of New France. But although they lost, their accomplishments were not small. The French were the first Europeans to explore deep within the North American continent. It was they, who, in a time when there were no automobiles or airplanes, in a land where it was not feasible to travel even by horse, forged a chain of communication and trade three thousand miles long from Montreal to the prairies of Saskatchewan, and it was done by the coureurs de bois and their voyageurs who paddled or carried heavy loads every inch of the way.

The French-occupied area of Rupert's Land was returned to the Hudson's Bay Company. Canada, which,

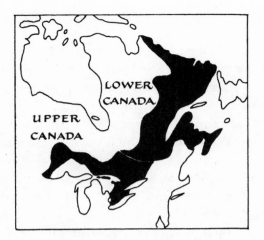

Canada in the 1700s. Upper Canada occupied higher ground (near the Great Lakes) than Lower Canada (along the St. Lawrence River and the Atlantic coast).

remember, at that time still consisted of only land near the St. Lawrence River and the lower Great Lakes, was ceded to Great Britain. (England and Scotland had by then joined to form Great Britain.)

The Nor'Westers

MOST OF THE coureurs de bois returned to France, leaving the door open to adventurous British businessmen—a great many of them Scots—who took over the Canadian fur trade headquartered in Montreal. Most of the voyageurs, many of them part Indian, remained and worked for the new Canadian traders, who followed much the same routes that the French had forged. They set up new trading posts wherever they saw fit, and like the French before them, cut off as much of the flow of fur to Hudson Bay as possible. Although the Hudson's Bay Company and the Canadian traders were all British, they were still rivals; Rupert's Land and Canada were separate British possessions.

In self-defense, the Hudson's Bay Company finally felt compelled to move into the interior of Rupert's Land and to set up its own inland trading posts. Beginning in 1720, and for about 100 years thereafter, Rupert's Land was scattered with rival trading posts, many of them rather closely paired, as traders from Hudson Bay and Montreal each tried to get the trade of the same Indians.

The competition of the one large Hudson's Bay Company with its short lines of communication made business difficult for the many small companies working the long distance out of Montreal. Therefore, in 1779, a few of the Montreal companies joined together in a temporary partnership that eventually grew into the North West Company.

By 1789, there were only two large competing fur companies in British North America—the Hudson's Bay Company in Rupert's Land and the North West Company operating out of Montreal in Canada. (In 1797, the XY Company split off from the North West Company, temporarily creating three companies, but the XY Company rejoined the North West Company in 1804.) The North West Company had some of the same advantages and disadvantages that the French traders had had—close and generally friendlier relations with the Indians but the extremely long (and continually lengthening), expensive line of communication that now stretched nearly across the continent.

The Nor'Westers, as the members of the company called themselves, therefore divided themselves into Montreal partners and wintering partners. The Montreal partners conducted business in Montreal, shipping furs out and ordering and receiving trade goods from England. The wintering partners stayed for several years in the western wilderness, spending each winter at one of their trading posts there. Every summer the Montreal partners and the wintering partners met at Grand Portage to make plans for the next year. To these meetings the wintering partners brought the furs they had obtained during the preceding year, and the Montreal partners brought the trade goods and supplies that the wintering partners would need during the next year.

The North West Company continued to press westward not only because of competition with the Hudson's Bay Company and because of the ever-present need to take the fur trade into new territory; there was, in addition, a new reason. Another nation had entered the North American fur trade some time before. A long time ago, Russian fur traders, trapping as they went, had worked their way across Siberia and had reached the Pacific Ocean. They started to explore the nearby islands off the Asian coast for a new source of furs. Some of these islands had populations of sea otters, marine mammals with one of the most luxurious and most desirable furs known.

In 1725, while the European nations were still searching hopefully for a convenient water route through or around North America to Asia, Tsar Peter the Great of Russia commissioned Danish explorer Vitus Bering to determine if there might be a land bridge between northeastern Asia and northwestern North America. The tsar hoped for a convenient way to settle a colony in North America. Bering, however, discovered the Bering Strait that separates the two continents. On a later expedition, Bering discovered the Aleutian Islands and the mainland of Alaska. This 1741 expedition brought back the information that these new lands had huge populations of sea otters and fur seals along their shores. It was not long

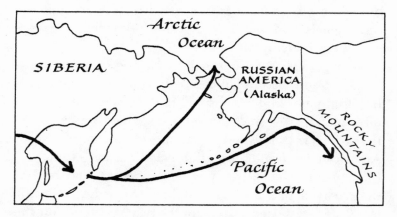

Early Russian explorations in the northern Pacific Ocean and the northwestern coasts of North America. The Russian fur trade in the Rocky Mountains caused the North West Company to search for the Northwest Passage.

before Russia had claimed the extreme northwestern part of North America. Russian America was approximately what the state of Alaska is today plus a southerly extension along the shore that, for a short time, reached almost to San Francisco.

Sea otters may have been the foremost reason for Russia's claiming this land, but, with the usual custom of fur hunters, the Russians soon had reduced drastically the size of the herds. They did have the good sense, however, to declare a moratorium on hunting sea otters until the herds had recovered sufficiently. In the meantime, they turned to beaver, which the Indians on the west coast of North America were willing to trade for Russian goods. In a short time, beaver pelts were traveling down the west side of the Rocky Mountains, from the mountain Indians who did the trapping to the coastal tribes who acted as middlemen between them and the Russians.

It was this trade that the North West Company wanted to stop, for they saw it diverting to the Russians furs that they wanted for themselves. If they could not stop all of this trade, they wanted to get as much of it as possible. And if they could not do that, they at least wanted the right to passage through Russian American territory to be able to ship their own furs from a Pacific port.

Although no one yet knew the size of North America, it was obvious that the North West Company must be getting close to the Pacific Ocean, and it would be much cheaper to send furs from a nearby west-coast port than to transport them by the long canoe trip all the way to Montreal. Finding the elusive Northwest Passage would solve some problems of the fur trade, and the Nor'Westers wanted to be the first to do it.

Hope that the Northwest Passage really existed was renewed by Peter Pond, a Yankee trader in the employ of the North West Company who had spent some time near Lake Athabaska from 1778 to 1779. There he heard from the Indians that a large river flowed westward from Great Slave Lake, a lake some distance to the north. Pond went there to investigate and ascertained that the river did exist; he even followed it westward for some distance and brought back a map he had made.

About the same time, British Captain James Cook was exploring the west coast of North America. There in Russian America he discovered what he believed (erroneously) to be the mouth of a large river flowing from the east. Cook's Inlet, as it was later called, and Peter Pond's river were at the same latitude.

Unfortunately, Pond was not a trained surveyor. Although his calculation of the latitude of the river was reasonably accurate, he estimated Great Slave Lake to be farther west than it really was. Not knowing of this error, the North West Company felt that so great a river flowing westward toward the mouth of another westward-

Alexander Mackenzie's explorations. His trip along the Mackenzie River was a disappointment. (See inset for the last hope of a Northwest Passage through North America.) His second trip along the Peace River, across the Rocky Mountains, and then down the western slopes successfully ended at the Pacific Ocean.

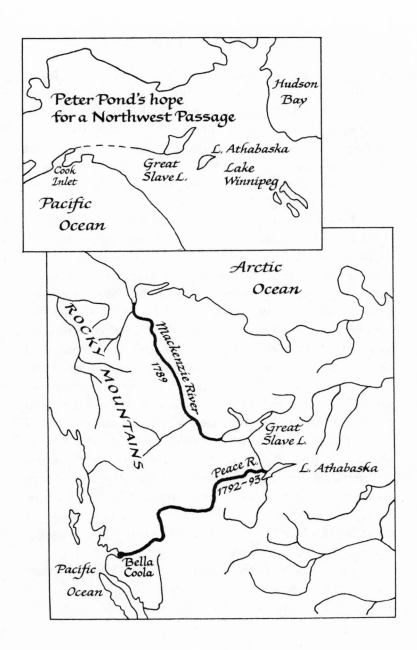

flowing great river a short distance away must almost certainly be part of that river. If the two rivers were one, then, here at last, must be the Northwest Passage. By right of discovery of its origin by Peter Pond, its mouth by Captain Cook, and the future exploration of the rest of the river by the North West Company, the company might win a distinct claim to the Northwest Passage even if it did go through Russian America.

Peter Pond might have been assigned to follow his river from Great Slave Lake, but he had the misfortune to be involved in a murder—the second one in a short time, at that—and the North West Company dismissed him. A young man named Alexander Mackenzie replaced him. In 1789, Mackenzie, who two years earlier had been assigned to the North West Company post on Lake Athabaska and had met and talked with Peter Pond there, assembled a small expedition and followed the river. From Great Slave Lake it flowed westward for about 200 miles, but, to Mackenzie's dismay, as it neared the Rocky Mountains it turned northwest and continued in that direction until it emptied not into the Pacific Ocean but into the Arctic Ocean. Mackenzie expressed his personal feelings in naming it the River of Disappointment. Later it was renamed the Mackenzie River in his honor. Though a disappointment in what it was meant to do for the Nor'Westers, the large river was a passageway into still more beaver country.

Alexander Mackenzie and the North West Company did not rest, however, for the news was about that the Hudson's Bay Company was actively seeking the Northwest Passage, too. Therefore, in 1792–1793, Mackenzie followed upstream the Peace River, which drained toward Lake Athabaska. This time he had somewhat better luck. The Peace led him and his expedition up into the Rocky Mountains, where waterfalls and tremendous rapids forced them into long portages. After reaching the Continental Divide, they found smaller rivers that eventually took them down the western slope of the Rocky Mountains and finally to the western sea. On July 22, 1793, Mackenzie arrived on the Pacific coast near what is now Bella Coola, British Columbia. His expedition was the first to cross the North American continent. (The famous Lewis and Clark expedition did not accomplish the crossing of the United States until 1805.)

Mackenzie had found the way to the Pacific Ocean, but no Northwest Passage. It was now clear that for 300 years Europeans had sought something that did not exist. There simply was no easy passage across the continent. But Mackenzie had completed one phase in the history of a great land. He and the trader-explorers before him had determined the dimensions of that country. From the Atlantic Ocean to Hudson Bay and the Arctic Ocean to the Pacific Ocean, it was the pursuit of the beaver that discovered, revealed, and measured this land.

The Competition Ends

BY NOW THE FUR TRADE was beginning to lose some of its vigor. For one thing, the success of reaching the Pacific Ocean meant that once the populations of fur-

bearers was drastically reduced in the newly explored
territories, the supplies of fur would drop. The fur trade
had always been one that lived beyond the ability of the
land to supply it. Trade had flourished only as long as it
could expand into fresh territory. Now the limit of available territory was known. Beyond that there would be
no expansion. From now on, the fur business would have
to manage better the animal populations on which it depended. Beaver and other fur-bearing animals could not
be hunted to extinction as in many parts of Europe and
Asia. That meant taking fewer animals each year and
meant smaller profits.

There was also the problem for the Nor'Westers of
maintaining supply lines that were longer than ever—up
to four thousand miles now. To make matters worse, thir-
teen of the British colonies on the Atlantic coast had re-
volted and formed the United States of America. In the
peace treaty at the end of the Revolutionary War, the
northern border that was set for the new country ran
down the middle of Lakes Ontario, Erie, and Huron and
then across the north shore of Lake Superior. As a result,
the North West Company lost some of its most important
forts and trading posts, many built by the French—Ni-
agara, Detroit, Michilimacinac, everything else around
Lake Michigan, and even Grand Portage—to the United
States.

In addition, both companies were suffering from the
wasteful competition of maintaining virtually side-by-
side posts. So in 1821, the Hudson's Bay Company and
the North West Company merged.

The Hudson's Bay Company brought to the new partnership Rupert's Land with its Hudson Bay ports. No longer would the long trip from Montreal be necessary. The North West Company brought to the partnership the vast western lands beyond Rupert's Land. The former Nor'Westers would work mostly in the western posts where they had the most experience, especially in the Mackenzie River system.

Until the merger, the North West Company had commanded the overwhelming portion of the fur trade, but the combined company took the name of the Hudson's Bay Company. The name carries with it the sense of adventure and excitement of wilderness living and hunting in the northern forests, but it does not reflect the long history of exploration that the name of the North West Company would have. The original Hudson's Bay people, after all, traveled far out from the bay only when they had to do so to meet the intrusion of the Nor'Westers into Rupert's Land.

Perhaps it was most appropriate, then, when, in 1867, all the British possessions north of the United States decided to unite, and they chose for the name of their country the Dominion of Canada—a remembrance of the early French colony and its coureurs de bois and voyageurs who blazed from Montreal a trail that the Nor'-Westers continued all the way to the Arctic and Pacific Oceans in pursuit of the beaver.

SUGGESTED
READINGS

Chapter 1
Horses in History

Braider, Donald. *The Life, History and Magic of the Horse.*
New York: Madison Square Press, Grosset & Dunlap,
1973.

Clabby, John. *The Natural History of the Horse.* New York:
Taplinger Publishing Company, 1976.

Dent, Anthony. *The Horse Through Fifty Centuries of Civilization.* New York: Holt, Rinehart, and Winston, 1974.

Haines, Francis. *Horses in America.* New York: Thomas Y.
Crowell Company, 1971.

Jankovich, Miklós. *They Rode into Europe: The Fruitful Exchange in the Arts of Horsemanship between East and West.* (Trans. Anthony Dent.) New York: Charles Scribner's Sons, 1971.

Chapter 2
Rats, Fleas, and the Black Death

Gottfried, Robert S. *The Black Death: Natural and Human Disaster in Medieval Europe*. New York: The Free Press, Macmillan Publishing Co., Inc., 1983.

Hatcher, John. *Plague, Population and the English Economy 1348–1350*. London: The Macmillan Press Ltd., 1977.

Langer, William L. *"The Black Death."* Scientific American 210(2): 114–122 (February 1964).

Ziegler, Philip. *The Black Death*. New York: The John Day Company, 1969.

Chapter 3
Beaver and the Exploration of Canada

Bryce, George. *The Remarkable History of the Hudson's Bay Company*, 2nd ed. New York: Burt Franklin, 1968.

Innis, Harold A. *The Fur Trade in Canada*, Rev. Ed. Toronto: University of Toronto Press, 1970.

Lavender, David. *Winner Take All*. New York: McGraw-Hill Book Company, 1977.

Sandoz, Mari. *The Beaver Men: Spearheads of Empire*. New York: Hastings House, Publishers, 1964.

In addition to the above readings, any complete history of Canada will have a section devoted to the fur trade.

INDEX